Struggle and Suffrage in Southend-on-Sea

Struggle and Suffrage in Southend-on-Sea

Women's Lives and the Fight for Equality

Dee Gordon

PEN & SWORD HISTORY
AN IMPRINT OF PEN & SWORD BOOKS LTD.
YORKSHIRE – PHILADELPHIA

First published in Great Britain in 2019 by
Pen & Sword HISTORY
An imprint of
Pen & Sword Books Limited
Yorkshire - Philadelphia

ISBN 978 1 52671 7 658

A CIP catalogue record for this book is available from the British Library

Typeset in 11.5/13.5 point Times NR MT by SRJ Info Jnana System Pvt Ltd.

Printed and bound in the UK
by TJ International Ltd, Padstow, Cornwall

Pen & Sword Books Limited incorporates the imprints of Atlas, Archaeology, Aviation, Discovery, Family History, Fiction, History, Maritime, Military, Military Classics, Politics, Select, Transport, True Crime, Air World, Frontline Publishing, Leo Cooper, Remember When, Seaforth Publishing, The Praetorian Press, Wharncliffe Local History, Wharncliffe Transport, Wharncliffe True Crime and White Owl.

For a complete list of Pen & Sword titles please contact
PEN & SWORD BOOKS LIMITED
47 Church Street, Barnsley, South Yorkshire S70 2AS, United Kingdom
E-mail: enquiries@pen-and-sword.co.uk
Website: www.pen-and-sword.co.uk

Or
PEN AND SWORD BOOKS
1950 Lawrence Rd, Havertown, PA 19083, USA
E-mail: Uspen-and-sword@casematepublishers.com
Website: www.penandswordbooks.com

Contents

Acknowledgements

The support of all those who have encouraged me to keep going when the research dried up (which happens!) has been invaluable – among these were Denise Oanes, Donna Lowe and Chris Sternshine. Specific help was given by Jennifer Simpson, the late Lynn Tait (for permission to quote from *The Tatler*), Lewis Herlitz, Carol Edwards, Judith Williams, Nigel Gayner, the staff at the Docklands Museum and the Women's Library, London, and at the Essex Record Office, Chelmsford. Photographs are from the author's collection, unless captioned otherwise.

Introduction

Between 1850 and 1950, the size and population of Southend-on-Sea grew in line with the changes in the lives of women. Their lifestyles, aspirations, education and healthcare all underwent dramatic changes locally and are detailed in the chapters which follow. 'Dramatic' does not understate the case when we remember that Victorian women had no rights over their children, lost control of their finances to their husbands on marriage, were unable to enter university, follow a profession or to vote. They could not even sue for divorce for adultery – although men could – and in the workplace, they had no protection from trade unions. The lives of working-class women in particular are almost ignored in social histories, and they do not feature in early portraits, other than perhaps as shadowy servants in the background. So while researching the invisible has proved difficult, it has proved fascinating – and quite an eye-opener. Enjoy!

CHAPTER ONE

Women in Education

In the nineteenth century, educational opportunities – especially for girls – were limited. In fact, when Canon King arrived in Leigh-on-Sea with his wife and six children in 1859, they were most likely to have been schooled at home until around the age of 8. This was when the five boys (two born later) were boarded out. Such was the general pattern for middle class girls at the time, seen as wives-in-training.

However, as the population of Southend-on-Sea and the surrounding areas (from Shoeburyness to Leigh-on-Sea) grew following the arrival of the railway in 1855, so did the demand for schooling, no longer regarded as the privilege of the middle and upper classes. Victorians began to realise that schools could offer a broader curriculum and better facilities for their children than relying solely on a governess. Leigh's Lady Olivia Sparrow endowed a national school in Leigh in 1834 and donated land for another in nearby Hadleigh in the 1850s, and Southend's Squire Scratton granted land in Old Southend, near The Castle public house, for a national school in 1853, which opened c.1855. Southchurch National School, as it was known, had been preceded by a 'Dame school' opposite Holy Trinity church (more of a cheap child-minding service) with the schoolmistress, Ann Arnold, also running the village shop and post office, and holding lessons at the back of her house. When the Southchurch school closed in 1948, no longer meeting the requirements of modern education, teacher Olive Goodale lost the job she had had for forty-five years (but she got another one pretty quickly in another school!). Another national school opened in 1868 in Prittlewell following local philanthropic donations of £500 towards the cost, and was described in the *Chelmsford Chronicle* of 29 May as a 'labour of love.' These schools provided elementary education to the children of the poor in accordance with the teaching of the Church of England. Although the latter closed less than twenty years later due to lack of funding, by then the Nonconformists British School in the High Street had 200 children on its roll. There were a few religious schools offering some basic educational skills, but these attracted little voluntary custom.

Those who were unlucky enough to spend time in Rochford workhouse should have received three hours each day in reading, writing, arithmetic and Christian religion, but there is little evidence that this took place – although girls probably avoided the cane, inflicted so readily on boys who stepped out of line. There is, however, a reference to a female industrial trainer being employed in 1882 at £25 p.a. to teach young women and girls the basics of needlework and domestic chores for domestic service. Access to local Sunday schools could also boost educational standards, with two-thirds of working-class children between the ages of 5 and 15 said to be attending these regularly by 1850.

The first 'school' in the South Shoebury area was a large single room on Church Street, financed by local philanthropists and fundraisers from 1862. Eleanor Cox was the assistant teacher while her father was the Head. The schoolroom was replaced a decade or so later by Hinguar Street School on the same site and in 1886, a Board School was erected close by, with Jessie Grater as the first schoolmistress. North Shoebury children attended the National School which had been established prior to 1818 in Great Wakering, a few miles away. In 1873 the Sutton and Shopland Council (then serving a rural community, since swallowed up by development to the north of Southend) opened a school in Sutton for local children who were not obliged to work in the fields. One of the teachers was Mrs Thackeray, the wife of a well-known local vicar, who specialised in needlework and art. All these teachers had to be versatile, however, not just in the variety of subjects they needed to teach, but as regards the age group they were teaching.

The *Southend Standard and Essex Weekly Advertiser* dated 27 March 1874 quotes a letter in *The Times* from a Miss Faithfull stating that:

> feminine education has been at least as useless as masculine, and decidedly more frivolous. The wretched girls who are turned out of school with a scanty provision of so-called accomplishments are too often as ill-fitted for domestic life as for profitable employments. The evil is not confined to any one class .... Whether women are hereafter to find their most appropriate sphere of action at home or abroad, we have no doubt that they might be infinitely better fitted for either class of duties by a more sensible and thorough system of education ... Every year there are more women in want of employment, and it is to be hoped that in time we shall begin to think of fitting them for employment.

Apart from this fairly traditional view, better schooling for girls had become a vital part of the movement towards female emancipation which had been increasing in momentum since the middle of the nineteenth century. The burden of single daughters had been difficult for many Victorian families to sustain, but girls were advised in Victorian publications (such as *Daughters of England*, by Sarah Stickney Ellis, 1843) that they should be content with being 'inferior to men – inferior in mental power in the same proportion that you are inferior in bodily strength'.

The school board for Prittlewell (including Southend) was set up in 1877 to replace religious schools and privately funded schools (such as Miss Felton's Infant School in Grosvenor Place) with board schools following the Elementary Education Act of 1870. This meant that children were for the first time obliged to attend between the ages of 5 and 10, though with the possibility of appeal, a possibility which disappeared in the 1880 Act which made it compulsory, with Attendance Officers employed to enforce the Act. In council minutes of 1903 there are details of attendance in the local schools, with bonuses being offered to Attendance Officers who improved the figures – which were mostly around eighty per cent – although Brewery Road School had achieved over ninety per cent, this result meaning that they were awarded a Challenge Shield. By 1917, women were being appointed as School Attendance Officers in Southend (according to the *Essex Newsman* 14 April 1917). Children from poor families could no longer fail to attend school because they were working to add to the family income; girls in particular had been regularly kept at home when mothers were overwhelmed by the amount of laundry or domestic chores they had to cope with.

Children from farming communities in areas such as Great Wakering had also been regularly kept from school to help at harvest time, and there are stories of children at Southchurch National School staying home for the pea-picking, or to go to Barnum and Bailey's Circus (1900)! It was a regular event at the turn of the century for parents to be fined for neglecting to send their children to school, but at least poor parents could be exempted from paying fees for education. Not that education was prolonged; the leaving age was raised from 10 to 11 in 1893 and, prior to 1877, pupil-teachers (teachers in training) could be as young as 13.

By 1888, the schools in Leigh-on-Sea initiated by Lady Olivia Sparrow were becoming too crowded, and a new school eventually opened in North Street in 1890 as Leigh Board School, to become Leigh North Street School at the beginning of the twentieth century. This could accommodate 200 girls and 200 boys – although they were kept separate, with a fence down the centre of the grounds.

The general approach to the education of girls is clear from an article in the *Southend Standard* of 12 February 1875. Here 'The Family Friend' points out that girls should be taught to: -

- cook a good meal of victuals and make the household bread
- darn stockings, sew on buttons and make shirts
- make their own dresses

- know the mysteries of the kitchen, dining room and parlour
- know the purchasing power of the pound
- live within their income, as the more they live beyond it the nearer they are to the poor-house
- do their own 'marketing' and to be particular in weighing or measuring their daily requirements
- prefer health to a fine appearance; to avoid tight lacing and wear thick warm shoes
- use strong, hard, practical common sense self-reliance
- spurn the attention of an intemperate or dissolute young man
- develop the habit of truth, sincerity, sprightness and the fear of the Lord
- marry for their welfare, to be a crown to their husbands and an honour to the grey hair of their parents.

Small private schools for a limited amount of girls flourished at the end of the nineteenth century in Southend. For example, Miss Jotham's school in Cashiobury Terrace (now a private dwelling) is mentioned in the memoirs of Warwick Deeping, a bestselling local author during the 1920s and 30s. His sister was a 'Jotham girl' and he gave her a letter to pass on to Lily Sternberg, a 'Venus' he had spotted (c.1885) among the sedate rows of Jotham schoolgirls at St John's church, which unfortunately resulted in no more than a polite thank-you note and multiple suppressed giggles. There is a list of these private schools in the 3 November 1903 issue of the *Southend Standard and Essex Weekly Advertiser*, thirteen in all, with 541 pupils in total, but with no reference to the sex of the pupils – although eight were run by single women, and another two by married or widowed women, indicating that the majority of pupils were also female. By 1905, all nine of the private schools listed had a 'Miss' as principal. These were in York Road, Westcliff Parade, Park Road, Alexandra Road, Hamlet Court Road and Southchurch Road. Some of these private schools were quite elitist – Leinster House School in Westcliff and Lancefield College in Alexandra Road both advertised their education as being provided for 'Daughters of Gentlemen'.

The Misses Jotham's 'Establishment for Young Ladies' (note: single women taking on responsible roles) is singled out for attention in a little booklet published in 1891, entitled *Where to Buy in Southend*, in the section regarding Education:

> The higher education of ladies is a specially interesting subject, and demands … considerably more tact and skill than is the case with the tuition of the opposite sex. The establishment conducted by the Misses Jotham has for 30 years been recognised as one affording exceptional opportunities for parents desiring to give their daughters the benefit of a high-class education combined with the comforts of their own houses. The lady principals have made the well-being of their young charges their life-study, and a graceful recognition of the value of their services is shown by their now having under their care daughters of former pupils, this being about the best recommendation possible. [There is] ample room for the healthful carrying on of the studies, and for the boarders' accommodation. That all important matter, sanitation, has been thoroughly dealt with, and to make sure that not the slightest ground for alarm may remain on this score, the whole system of drainage has been overhauled at great expense, and the latest scientific improvements adopted. The general course of instruction consists of the various branches of a useful and liberal English education based on religious principles – French, German, the pianoforte, violin, singing, drawing, and dancing being extra subjects, taught by visiting London professors and a resident foreign governess. Calisthenics are also taught by a Sergeant Drill Master. Pupils are prepared for the College of Preceptors' Local Examination, also for the Local Examination of the Royal Academy of Music … terms for boarders and day-pupils are based on a moderate scale, and the domestic arrangements of the establishment are in every way satisfactory, and

> we need only add that the situation of the place is both picturesque and healthy, and there is good opportunity for sea-bathing, which is freely permitted under careful surveillance.

Following an advertisement in the *Southend Standard* on 18 December 1891, promoting the 'advantages of higher modern education', Brightbe School for Girls, a Higher Education facility, opened a month later. The school took both day and boarding students, its principal in 1899 being 'Miss Elizabeth Bannester, B.A. London', who moved into the premises then in Avenue Road, Southend – note her degree, at a time when such women were called 'blue stockings' (not intended as a compliment). She had previously been teaching French at evening classes in Southend before becoming Joint Head of Brightbe in 1893, and was apparently always to be seen in her black academic gown. Rosa Pagenoff was one of those in 1899 who were 'allowed' to take Cambridge school exams to see if they could compete with boys without developing 'brain fever': she was successful. This college advertised regularly in the *Southend Standard and Essex Weekly Advertiser* around the turn of the century, boasting of its examination successes in 'London Matriculation, University Locals, College of Preceptors, Incorporated Society of Musicians, and Trinity College of Music.' [The names of students listed in 1900 are, incidentally, rather predictable – ninety-nine per cent were Edith, Winnie, Dolly, Hettie or Nellie!] In 1902, Brightbe moved to larger premises in Crowstone Road, Westcliff, and became Alexandra College, 'for the daughters of Gentlemen'. The College prospered under Miss Bannester, with her co-principal, Rose Brown, taking over on her death in 1914. Miss Brown has been described as 'a stickler for deportment and etiquette', a tall woman with a commanding, 'straight-backed ample figure [and] … great dignity and poise', who encouraged students to 'cultivate a silvery laugh'. This was a very different approach to her pioneering, academic predecessor who had educated her girls to prepare them for the world of work rather than womanly accomplishments – although it has to be said that many parents agreed more with Miss Brown than Miss Bannester: a sign of the times.

The first local technical school was the 'Day Science School' in Clarence Road which opened in 1895 for boys and girls, with successes acclaimed annually. A sample celebration was at The Pavilion (then at the shore-end of the Pier) in 1898, with some interesting information regarding the prize distribution given in the *Southend Standard and Essex Weekly Advertiser* (1 December issue). Winifred Cox was named as 'first among all the girls from Essex presented for the Major Scholarships', gaining £45 for three years, with the next girl, Jessie Clark, also a Southender, second in the same competition and gaining a similar scholarship. The fact that there were no boys' names mentioned in connection with this scholarship examination was explained by the fact that, unfortunately, none of their boys had been able to secure scholarships – they 'just missed' out. Prizes were given by the mayoress, and the venue was described as 'crowded'.

The account of this event is enlivened by the speech given by a Miss Page, headmistress of Skinner's Company's School in London, who had presumably travelled to Southend specifically for the presentations. Asserting that 'men and women made the nation', she pointed out that both must be 'equally cared for'. She refers to a time 'twenty years ago', when the 'system of a girl's education was designed to omit every element of backbone strength. There was singing, the ability to make a noise on the pianoforte, a little painting, and some fancy needlework and with these education was considered complete.' She then pointed out that:

> boys and girls were capable of reason, observation, memory, the ability to grasp main principles; also to distinguish them from details and to be careful in regard to the detail work, and if all these were left out of a girl's education, it would be impossible to get women of real strength in the community.

The response of the audience is not recorded. Miss Page went on to stress that 'the girl, when she became a woman, must either marry, live upon an income that had been left her, or go into the world to win one for herself', and proclaimed it to be a duty on the part of the nation 'to educate the girls so that their higher qualities might be brought out'.

Southend Committee minutes for 1899 mention four of five scholarships for further education being granted to female students. The technical schools' prizegiving in December of that year – another well attended event, this time at the Empire Theatre – has a long list of the scholarships gained, with the Chairman, Mr Langton, referring to the 'Southend Technical Girls' as pre-eminent and 'beyond criticism'. Improved schooling for girls was an important part of the movement towards female emancipation at a time when there were not enough husbands for Victorian women, who outnumbered single men by around three to one in 1850; even by the census of 1921 for the area of Rochford Hundred (which included Southend), there were 14,000 more women than men. This meant women needed to earn an independent living, rather than rely on the income of a husband. What kind of living that was is typified by the separate lessons on offer in Brewery Road School in 1892 – boys offered gardening and girls offered sewing and cooking, with separate parts of the playground allocated.

It is important to remember that Victorian society generally considered it unfeminine to pursue intellectual pursuits to avoid the danger of women usurping the natural (!) intellectual superiority of the male. It had even been reported that too much study had a damaging effect on the ovaries, hence the emphasis on accomplishments rather than academia. For instance, a letter in *The Times* in 1872 announced that females ran the risk of 'becoming sterile' if they followed a course of higher education and puberty was felt to be a particularly 'dangerous' time for study. This had less of an impact on the working classes at that time, because girls were usually already working – in factories or as domestics – by the time they reached puberty. On 8 June 1907, the *Essex Newsman* reported on plans for a creche to be opened in Southend for the children of poor working women – a welcome move.

Education in the town, as no doubt elsewhere, was affected by outbreaks of infectious diseases. Examples include St Mary's (the convent school which had preceded St Bernard's) which could not open for a month in 1899 due to 'influenza prostrating the two chief professional teachers', and London Road Infants School closed in 1911 for three weeks following a measles outbreak. There was also the requirement for young women to help out at home as when Miss 'A. Standing' was sent home from Hinguar School in Shoeburyness in 1900 – according to the school log book – to 'do the work of the house as the mother is obliged to assist her husband in the brickfield as he is unable to get a barrow load'. Pupils at this school, it seems, had very protective parents – there is a reference in 1903 to parents complaining about 'any punishment whatsoever' meted out, and to notes written to teachers 'in objectionable language'. Even bad weather could have a detrimental effect on education in the days before central heating. West Leigh School, for instance, which had opened in 1913 to accommodate 278 juniors and 171 infants, closed regularly in 1916 due to cold weather and a lack of fuel. Interestingly, when the Education Committee met in February 1908 to discuss the Education (Provision of Meals) Act of 1906, although they reported that 200 families (with 300 children) had assistance in some way or other, comparatively few attended school 'without food', therefore it was not necessary to put into force any part of the Act. On the other hand, a committee was set up in 1911 to raise money to pay for boots when 187 children arrived at Hinguar School with no shoes.

In 1902, a new technical college at Victoria Circus was opened by Lady Warwick who had been running a school in science and agriculture at her estate near Chelmsford. She was interested in schools funded by local taxes and open to girls as part of a wider movement for higher education and entry to the professions by women. There was also some practical – if predictable – instruction for young women given at a Special

Instruction Centre in Queen's Road where Cookery and Laundry were on the agenda in 1908. However, early discrimination within female education continued – for instance, in 1914, some girls at Alexandra College were withdrawn from classes in 'vigorous subjects', in case they became 'unwomanly'. At least by then girls had access to tennis and cricket and to a gym which had been added in 1913. Things were moving on from an emphasis on needlework, which had been regarded as an essential for all classes of female – to sew and repair their own clothes, to save money, to make toys or samplers or household linen.

The 1902 Education Act abolished school boards and created local education authorities (LEAs), leaving Essex County Council in control of the existing schools and of the building of eight new ones in Prittlewell, central Southend, Southchurch, Leigh-on-Sea and Westcliff-on-Sea, with St Christopher's School for children with special needs opening in 1906. This was the year when women started to feature in the Minutes of the Education Committee, with a Mrs Osborn in situ by February, and Miss Blanche Wells appointed to the mistress-ship of a Special Class for Defective Children in May – which may have been the catalyst for St Christopher's. In this connection, there is also a 1906 reference to the necessity for 'a woman to be engaged to meet the children [described again as 'defective'] alighting from the trams at Victoria Corner, take them to school and see to their return after school'. Finally, a few local women were on committees influencing local education, and keeping an eye on female teachers – the headmistress of London Road Infants' Department, Miss Haigh, was granted leave of absence by the Committee for four months in December 1911 on account of a 'complete breakdown'. Note that the regulation which meant that women teachers had their appointment terminated on marriage was waived for the period of the First World War. The main concern of the use of temporary female teachers who replaced male staff joining HM Forces seems to have been regarding the levels of discipline rather than the teaching skills.

Chalkwell Hall School in Westcliff joined the growing number of educational establishments in the area in 1909, initially for infant, junior and senior children. A special 1984 edition of the school magazine *The Tatler*, recording memories of the early years, refers to the limitations of long-handled pens with scratchy nibs, and the 'inkwell monitor' responsible for re-filling the inkwells and delivering them, a messy task. There was also a monthly laundry day during the First World War years when girls were taught the pre-washing-machine arts of sorting, boiling, rinsing, blueing, starching, ironing and 'guffering' – using a heated tong to crimp up the frills. (Chalkwell Hall was one of those that remained open during the First World War but evacuated hundreds of children and teachers to Derbyshire during the Second World War to continue their education.) In the 1930s, one ex-pupil of Chalkwell Hall remembers learning to knit on extra thick needles with extra thick, stiff wool. After the Second World War, another pupil recalls 'drill' (a forerunner of Physical Education or PE) and learning passages of the Bible by heart, with large classes of more than forty children.

Most of these new schools provided for boys and girls alike, but in 1910 St Bernard's Girls Catholic School opened with 120 day girls in Westcliff, having for several decades been an orphanage and school for girls run by German nuns. As a school, it had boasted within the pages of its parish magazine prior to 1906 that it was 'one of the best Catholic schools in Essex', taking up 'the cause of poor children [mainly girls] of all degrees in order to provide for their education'.

Three years later the first High School for Girls in Southend opened in Boston Avenue, with 300 pupils, introducing opportunities beyond the domestic sphere with its science laboratory and facilities for hockey, cricket, lawn tennis, netball and rounders. This was quite alien for girls who had previously been rubbing shoulders with male students. Sport was beginning to feature strongly for girls in education, and sports days would include such joys as the tug-of-war and sack race. Emblazoned in stained glass in the main corridor were the words: 'So enter that thou mayest become daily more learned. So depart that thou mayest become more useful to thy Country and to mankind.' Discipline here was regarded as strict, and girls could collect conduct marks for forgetting a ruler or a book, or a disorder mark for talking out of turn, with three marks meaning a visit to the headmistress. The wartime head was Miss Lewis, who was obviously aware of the difficulties that young women would incur on leaving school to face a world with less men available to marry – she is said to have exhorted her students 'to choose such careers as teaching or medical work which would absorb our whole being'. She was also apparently convinced that all women would soon get the vote and wanted her girls to 'enter fully' into their new responsibilities. One student (in *Tales Out of School*) remembers Miss Lewis as 'a queenly woman with a wonderful presence, tall and slim, endowed by nature with good looks … luminous eyes and musical voice … inner radiance … [and] natural authority'. Another remembers one particular teacher, Miss Cleveland, the English mistress at Southend High School during the First World War, as 'tall and willowy', prone to wearing 'such a tight hobble skirt that she had difficulty in stepping from the classroom floor on to the platform where the staff desk was'. Others recall school dinners – sausages cut in three, and suet pudding. When Miss Lewis left the school in 1918, shortly before the November armistice, her replacement, Miss Swann (later known as The Bird), immediately consigned all the German books to the back of the top shelf of the book cupboard and announced: 'There is no Germany, no German language. I never want to hear the word German in the school.' The Bird has been described as 'a dragon … immensely tall and poker-like', but also as 'selfless', and offering 'wise guidance'.

The Hinguar School (Shoeburyness) log-book has some fascinating observations about teachers over the years. In 1907, a Miss Annie Clouting commenced work on 2 September but was absent with influenza two days later, and was cautioned for unsatisfactory work after just a month. In 1922, Miss Knott was recorded as 'almost hopeless', and in 1924, 20-year-old Miss Duke fared even worse when overwhelmed by responsibility for a class, resulting in her description as 'hopeless'. Miss Cox in 1928 received many complaints (presumably from parents) and actually went absent after 'wounding' a male pupil – suggesting a different reaction to pressure perhaps. Another memorable teacher was at Richmond Avenue Primary in 1947 – a Miss Davey, remembered by some as being 'very short, very round, very feisty, very blonde and wearing bright make-up in contrast to post-war grey'. Similarly, West Leigh Schools' record has details of Miss Durrant being absent in June 1915 due to 'severe shock through being in a train crash', and of Mrs Hammond being absent the same month, 'owing to the death of her husband killed in action on the 25th May'.

Both wars, of course, meant considerable disruption for education in the town for boys and girls alike, although, on balance, looking at memoirs, the boys seemed to 'enjoy' the experience more than the girls! At the start of the First World War, Southend Education Committee made an order compelling schoolchildren to remain in their classrooms during air raids, the last of which was on Whit Sunday 1918. At Alexandra College, girls took their most treasured possessions down to the kitchens overnight during Zeppelin raids. At Southend High School for Girls, the benches in the physics laboratory proved useful to dive under on such occasions, with tea cosies grabbed to cover any exposed heads. Pupils in the town got involved by growing vegetables or making crutches, bed screens and splints for the Red Cross. Schoolgirls at Chalkwell School knitted mittens which they sent to France even though – because their knitting styles were different – the mittens were odd sizes. A thank-you letter in March 1915, however, assured them that they were 'just the thing to keep our hands warm these cold mornings'. Gladys Wayland from North Street School in Leigh, age 7, was awarded the Empire Day Certificate for providing an unknown amount of eggs (one egg equating to a meal!) to the war-wounded patients at Queen Mary's Hospital, which reverted to its role as a luxury seafront hotel after the war.

The Girl Guide movement came into its own during the war years. There were more than 1,500 Girl Guides in Southend in spite of thousands of children being evacuated, working with the ARP and acting as hospital messengers. Older girls – Rangers – assisted the Women's Voluntary Services (WVS) and the Red

Cross, and the younger Brownies helped out collecting clothes and toys for local youngsters. This movement passed on useful skills which young women were unlikely to learn elsewhere, and gave some a taste of a different world. Young women who joined organisations such as the early Land Army in the First World War would also experience a very different type of education – milking cows, churning butter, ploughing, riding a horse-and-trap, even shooting local vermin in rural areas around Southend, including rabbits. By the time of the next war they were also driving mechanised tractors and threshing machines in areas such as Wakering and Potton Island, just a few miles from Southend.

Despite some of the boarders returning to their homes, Alexandra College was one of the schools that remained open during the First World War – although the school uniform was abandoned for the war years. When the boarders returned at the end of the war, they could enjoy afternoon teas with Miss Brown at her home, and listen to her reading for an hour or so. The post-war years saw continued growth in the limits of education – ancient history was on the curriculum, a philatelic society, cycling club and reading club appeared, admittedly alongside more feminine pursuits such as ballroom dancing. There was also the introduction of the first male teacher in 1919 – Sergeant Young – who was brought on board to teach gymnastics, and did so in a way that reflected his military background.

By the 1920s, the curriculum at Southend High School for Girls included Latin, phonetics, European languages and music, and the ethos of the school can be estimated by such insights as their employing a female caretaker. The female teachers did not take a softly-softly approach to their pupils as might have been expected in some quarters, with such individuals as Miss Foley being remembered for her favourite expression – 'I'll knock you into the middle of next week!' Miss Foley was not the only teacher to use physicality – there was a Miss Wright at West Leigh School in 1924 who 'clumped you across the head with a ruler if you misbehaved'. In *What An Education*, published by West Leigh Junior School in 2003, Miss Wright was described as having a 'grey face, grey hair and grey clothes', the publication is hardly more complimentary when also describing Miss Howe in the 1940s with her 'Harris tweed, thick Lyle stockings and heavy brogues'.

Middle-class female pupils were expected to be particularly well-behaved both in and out of school. Those in Alexandra College were not allowed to speak to boys in nearby schools, and those at Southend High School for Girls were similarly banned when in uniform, which included a pleated blue serge gymslip, unpopular round hats and black stockings. Before the First World War, girls with long hair had to have it plaited and hanging down their backs – hanging the plaits in front was not allowed, and nor were hair slides or any sort of jewellery. Not only that, but bobbed hair had to be hidden under a bathing cap for cookery lessons to avoid hair in the cakes or batters. Fast forward to the 1930s, and some girls at this same school were scolded in assembly for eating ice-cream at Rossi's in the High Street while in uniform, but after the Second World War, enforcing such decorum outside the schools became more and more difficult.

In 1927, Alexandra College was sold on to Miss Florence Le Page, keen to raise the academic standard and send girls to university, which she achieved in the 1930s. She and her two sisters (Miss Winifred and Miss Ethel), who also taught at the College, were known to wear very similar ankle-length silky dresses. To cope with expansion, Miss Florence acquired another premise close by, also in Crowstone Road, necessitating the purchase of galoshes to walk from one building to another without damaging the College floors! Several other teachers joined the staff during the 1930s, with the curriculum being extended to include such diversity as Poetry, Elocution, Greek Dancing, Violin and Percussion classes (in addition to the long-standing piano classes) and Biology. When Sergeant Young retired, a new gym mistress, Miss Caister, held a vigorous remedial session each morning to improve round shoulders and flat feet, and was keen on including ornamental marching in the annual sports' day (accompanied by an elderly piano). Early morning bathing was not popular in the glacial waters of the nearby Thames. Miss Le Page arranged for career articles to be published in the annual school magazine before the Second World War – teaching, secretarial skills, beauty culture, and angora-wool farming were all given space. However, although quite forward thinking, in 1935 she was taken aback when one student asked for a half day off on her seventeenth birthday to take her driving test; Miss Le Page thought it was something to do with the Girl Guides!

Westcliff High School for Girls opened in 1931 followed by Wentworth School for Girls in 1932. Sadly, it was not until the 1944 Education Act that secondary education became free, with girls charged before this even for things like the use of glasses and plates – even if they brought their own lunch! However, there were scholarship opportunities for the poor, male or female, and girls held their own with the boys in availing themselves of these opportunities. Small private schools with boarders in addition to day pupils were still operating locally in the run-up to the Second World War. One, Tower House School in Salisbury Road, Leigh-on-Sea, was described in *Leighway* magazine as offering drama, nature study, verse speaking, elocution and shorthand-typing, the typewriter an instrument of dramatic social change, already offering real freedom of choice for so many women.

The girls at Southend High School welcomed a more progressive headmistress in 1937, Miss Cowell, who almost immediately banished the hated thick black stockings. However, she was soon to be involved in the building of air raid shelters in the grounds, and with getting the girls and teachers ready for the train journey to Mansfield in June 1940 after it was announced that all schools on or near the coast from Great Yarmouth to the Isle of Wight were being evacuated. They did not return to Boston Avenue until October 1942, their education having continued in Mansfield, some having fond memories of their foster families and billets, others less so. The teaching staff returned to fire-watching duty in trousers and helmets, replacing the men, with bombing raids continuing in the town, meaning that the trenches dug pre-war on the hockey field were put to good use.

More schools closed during the Second World War than the first, with several being bombed. As many as 8,000 schoolchildren, along with their teachers, were evacuated to less urban areas on 8 June 1940, this caused staffing problems and led to the recruitment of temporary teachers, including married women who had been previously excluded. There was a trial run teaching some of the remaining children in the homes of those (mainly female) remaining teachers but this seemed too impractical to continue long term. The girls at Alexandra College were evacuated en masse to Sidbury in Devon, but not all of the teachers, many of whom became involved in war work. It continued in Sidbury for a while after peace was declared, but the girls slowly returned to Westcliff, to other schools, leaving Miss Le Page and her sisters behind until it finally closed in 1959.

After the Second World War there was a distinct improvement in educational facilities for young women in the town – with the Municipal College which opened in 1908 including hairdressing alongside its more macho technical subjects by 1947. Southend High School for Girls introduced a range of extra-curricular societies in the 1920s – the classical society, cercle Francais, geographical society, gardening club, and social service guild, together with such events as the poetry competitions, followed in the 1930s by an arts society and a choir. While this offered some progress, girls could still have their powder-puffs confiscated if discovered!

Summing up then, both young women and young men benefited from a plethora of Education Acts between 1870 and 1944 where universal compulsory education was introduced, became free, and where the leaving age was gradually increased. (The GCE followed soon after – in 1951). Not all children might have appreciated the benefits of this revolution, of course! From the Edwardian era onwards, teenage girls had more opportunities for scholarships, for further education and for university places, the first generation of females whose education was on a par with males.

CHAPTER TWO

Women in the Workplace

With the rise in the education of females, it is not surprising that female employment also came to prominence. However, given the necessity for so many single women to earn a living, the choices throughout the nineteenth century were very dependent on class. Middle-class teenage women who had received a private education could train as teachers in local schools, or could join a middle- or upper-class family as a governess. Young working-class women with very basic educational skills would become unpaid carers for their siblings or parents, or find low-paid work in domestic service or agriculture – Southend was far more agricultural in the 1850s than its twenty-first-century façade reveals. Twenty years later, the latter option was diminishing with the onset of the industrial revolution when 'female' tasks such as weeding and stone picking became obsolete. In fact, the Agricultural Workers Union (formed in 1872) opposed the employment of women because they 'took work from men, kept wages down and destroyed family life'. Trades unions were also, in general, hostile to women's suffrage, and various historians consider the reasons for this as being a mixture of fear, jealousy and pride. (The inspiration for the formation of unions, especially for women, was the Bryant and May's Match Girls Strike of 1888 in the East End of London, led by Annie Besant, the women's rights activist and suffragette.)

One change for female workers, nationally and locally, came around 1860 when the image of nursing as an unskilled working-class profession changed and began to attract ladies of birth and education (note that the London School of Medicine for Women was founded in 1874). This would have been welcomed by Southend's first hospital, the Victoria Hospital, established in Warrior Square in 1888 with just eight beds and two cots, and replaced by a more suitably sized building in Prittlewell Chase in 1932. This provided a children's block, outpatients, X-ray facilities, laboratories, operating theatres and maternity wards. Nurses had the benefit of a purpose-built nurses' home with a library, leisure rooms and lecture room, with extra facilities such as a sporting club. During the Second World War, training for nurses at the new hospital was increased – and many even learned German to treat the intake of Luftwaffe!

Nurses were also needed at Rochford workhouse, built in 1837 to replace smaller workhouses dotted around the Southend area (including those at Leigh, Shoebury, and Prittlewell). Over the first thirty years of its history, just two nurses were employed, and both had long careers – a Mrs Bloxam was there for twenty years. Another long-term employee, Mrs Hinton, arrived at the workhouse as an inmate, described as a 'young half-caste widow of a soldier who brought her home from India'. She stayed on as an unpaid servant of the Guardians of the workhouse, but moved on to being a cook at another workhouse for which she was paid a salary; the Guardians realised too late what they had lost. Mrs Hinton, at least, knew her value, and perhaps her 'rights'. By 1900, the workhouse was really struggling to hang on to its nursing staff. A Nurse Whitehead stayed just three days, returning to her home in Newcastle, with no reason given, necessitating the employment of a temporary nurse. The board of the Rochford Guardians were reported in the *Southend Standard and Essex Weekly Advertiser* of 6 September as being in agreement that the low salary was part of the problem, and they would soon 'get sick' of advertising the vacancy! Restrictions imposed, which included the necessity of being single or an 'unencumbered widow' with some midwifery experience, did not help with recruitment. (Incidentally, even in 1913, the Health Committee reported that they needed to increase the salary for the TB Nurse and Health Visitor from £70 p.a. to £90 p.a. rising to £110 p.a., because they were having difficulty recruiting, resulting in three suitable candidates applying.)

While it seems that public opinion generally objected to the notion of working women, which was perceived as unfeminine, nineteenth-century women became entrepreneurial from necessity, needing to provide for their families with no help from the state, especially if widowed or with absentee or incapable husbands. Admittedly, no longer could local women such as Elizabeth Little earn a living by smuggling in goods from France, or Sarah Moore collect pennies from sailors on the wharf at Leigh-on-Sea by threatening them with death at sea if they did not pay up! But by the 1830s, there had been three female landladies at The Crooked Billet in the High Street in Leigh, with landladies there in 1865 and 1900 taking over when their respective husbands died. Women of tougher mettle were known to have been working in local brickfields in the 1860s and 1870s, and there were elderly women then in Leigh who charged fishermen to boil the shrimps they caught – at a penny or less per gallon. Such women did not think about their rights; they knew themselves to be equal in all but status, and they had more important things to think about – like feeding their children. Working-class women at the beginning of the twentieth century had to work or starve, living in sub-standard housing with inadequate food and accepting any work that came their way for little more than a pittance.

While service was a natural choice for working class women in Southend, as elsewhere in Victorian England, there was a form of progression through the ranks to heading up the household or the kitchen. Jane Elizabeth Chennery held the office of cook at the Royal Hotel for twenty-five years from 1855 until her death in 1880 aged 54, following a short-lived bronchial infection. The *Southend Standard* and *Chelmsford Chronicle* (both of which mistakenly referred to her as Chinnery) referred to her respectively as being 'an old and valued servant … much respected', and 'well known to visitors' at the Royal. These descriptions, and her headstone at St John's Church nearby dedicated by fellow servants and friends, shows that this was no ordinary cook – in more ways than one, perhaps, with the *Standard* mentioning that it took eight men to carry her extra large coffin!

Not all cooks were held in such high esteem. Mary Shields of Prittlewell Passage tried to sue her ex-employer, Henry Dettmar of Clifton Terrace, for 18*s* 4*d* – being a month's wages in lieu of notice – in October 1881. She had been engaged for a trial period only, as she had no 'character' or confirmed experience, but was dismissed after just two days when Mr Dettmar knew her to be drunk 'by her speech', as reported in the *Southend Standard* in its Southend County Court pages (7 October). The *Chelmsford Chronicle* had a more detailed account of Mary's being 'tipsy' on her first night, quoting the housemaid, Sarah Minter, who described her as 'drunk when she came in'. The daughters of the house also confirmed that Mary appeared to be intoxicated; His Honour J.T. Ardy, felt there was a very good reason for Mr Dettmar's decision and the case was dismissed.

Before the 1870 Married Women's Property Act, any money earned or inherited by a woman automatically became that of her husband once she was married, as did her assets, e.g., property. So Eliza Sharp was taking a risk by earning money from her donkey rides in the 1840s. She plied for hire outside the Ship Hotel on the seafront when her husband was proprietor, but could be seen with her donkeys around the town. Eliza did not have the easiest life – in 1883, the *Essex Newsman* refers to her being summoned for 'unlawfully acting as the driver of two asses', for which she was fined 20*s* plus 12*s* costs or fourteen days' imprisonment. She was in trouble again in 1905, featuring in the same newspaper – this time summoned for 'allowing two donkeys to stray on the Highway'. In her defence, she stated that she 'did not have two donkeys, one's only a baby'! The response is revealing: 'You will be fined 2*s* 6*d* each donkey and costs 3*s* 6*d* as usual', although Eliza again objected: 'You have never charged full price for a baby before.'

In other parts of the UK there were growing opportunities in factories, offering more freedom, companionship, and an escape from domesticity, but this was less evident in seaside towns like Southend, which has never been an industrial town. Added to that, there was an article in the *Southend Standard and Essex Weekly Advertiser* of 13 June 1873, quoting the Nine Hours Bill and the Shop Hours Regulation Bill outlined in *The Times:* Millicent Garrett Fawcett (a leading suffragist and campaigner) pointed out here that if it is 'illegal to employ women in a factory more than nine hours a day or in a shop for more than 10 hours a day, of course every employer will as far as possible avoid using female labour however well motivated the thinking behind the Bill'. She stressed that 'every obstacle that is put in the way of the honest labour of women leads to swell the number of the thousands who are making a living that is not honest in the streets of our towns and cities'.

There was a fascinating article published in *Urban History* in 2014 by Dr David Churchill which gives some data regarding working-class women in Southend in both 1871 and 1891. His detailed research shows that there were more domestic servants employed in the affluent Clifftown area of Southend, with its imposing housing (where the 'new' town was developed following visits from Princess Caroline and the coming of the railway in the mid-nineteenth century), than in the 'old' town at the bottom of the cliffs, which had originated as a fishing community. This not only reinforces the east/west class divide of the town, but also shows the high proportion of working class women employed in domestic service compared to those employed, for example, as shop assistants.

From 1871 to 1911, the proportion of women nationally in service slipped below forty per cent and slipped even further by 1931. This was partly due to some families no longer being able to hang on to cheap labour in the form of servants working up to 100 hours per week. Sadly, it has been impossible to find a diary of any particular servant in the area (poor levels of literacy no doubt to blame), but it seems they were often a valued part of the family, if the letters of Juliana Stuart King of the rectory at nearby Leigh-on-Sea are anything to go by. They reveal titbits such as a reference in October 1887 to her new maid 'M', praising her dusting but baffled by her propensity for arranging items askew, which M regarded as 'elegant'. Mrs King also mentions the gifts granted to servants in their old age, which included whisky, a 'flannel petticoat' or even a few shillings. Similarly, doctor's wife Mary Willing in Wakering kept a diary from 1865 referencing her discomfort if one of her servants was poorly, but was able to engage a replacement immediately if one was to leave. In 1861, less valued workers had gained protection from assault by employers thanks to the Offences Against the Person Act.

Women who 'farmed out' their babies (often illegitimate, with the Victorian social stigma attached) for a few pence a week – enabling them to work – were not, however, protected from those who just spent the money and mistreated the youngsters. This Victorian scandal featured in *Essex Newsman* of 25 October 1913, when two women were arrested for 'baby farming' in Inverness Avenue, Westcliff. They were summoned for 'wilful ill treatment and neglect in a manner likely to cause unnecessary suffering and injury to health'. Even though some of these children ended up dead, and some of the women were hanged as a result, the practice was commonplace until at least the First World War. This particular case was reported in rather sensational detail in the *Southend Standard* of 30 October. The three children concerned were 'farmed' out because the mother was in 'delicate health' and the father was working in Canada. An NSPCC Inspector found them – Alma Wood, aged 5, Norman Wood, aged 4, and Ronald Wood, aged 3 – tied together in uncomfortable conditions without ventilation. They were removed to safety, and Lydia Goldsworthy and Florrie Peak were prosecuted for neglect and for using knotted stockings and straps (produced in evidence) to ill-treat the children.

From around 1860, Nelson Street and Alexandra Street were busy shopping areas for more affluent families, convenient for those residents of the new Clifftown Estate near Southend Central station. Garons was the forerunner for the development of the shops in the High Street, with many smaller shops following suit from 1885. This meant that there was plenty of work for female shop assistants, but note 'assistants' rather than 'proprietors'. Carol Edwards's research for *The Old Town, Leigh on Sea,* revealed a Mrs J. Shaw running a shop in the High Street in Leigh-on-Sea in 1881 – a draper's selling tartans, guernseys and scarves. In 1913, there is a record of a Mrs M. Phillips owning a draper's in Southend's Pleasant Road, in that she was fined 10*s* plus 4*s* costs for failing to close on Wednesday afternoon, 29 January, 'in pursuance of the Southend-on-Sea weekly half holiday' (the prosecution minuted by the Health Committee). The town's offices prior to 1850 were mainly staffed by men, but over the next seven decades the Civil Service and Post Office slowly opened up to women.

Local women, from unidentified social backgrounds, can be seen to be earning a living in diverse ways just by looking at the local *Kelly's* directories pertaining to the Victorian period. In 1882, it is obvious that Southend is growing as a resort, with fifty-four married and thirteen single women – or spinsters to use the term of the period – listed as running 'lodging houses' in and around the town centre and seafront. There were a couple of shopkeepers, a midwife, a handful of dressmakers, a couple running 'ladies' schools', a druggist, laundress, stationer, draper and a Mrs Mary Cripps running a refreshment room on Marine Parade.

Twelve years later, the larger 1894 edition of *Kelly's* for Rochford (north of Southend), reveals a Mrs Eliza Asbey of The Square as a plumber, glazier and decorator; Mrs Lucy Bishop as a dressmaker in Church Street; Mrs Eliza Long as a baker in North Street; Mrs Mary Ann Tasker, an ironmonger; Mrs Sophia Thorogood a shopkeeper in Church Street, and a Mrs Emma Hedgecock running a 'fancy repository' in South Street. In Shoeburyness (east of Southend) there are two schoolmistresses listed – Mrs Eleanor Cox at the national school and Miss Ellen Alston at the local board school for infants, plus Mrs Annette Baldwin heading up the Shoeburyness Tavern, Mrs Mary Carr the laundry, with Mrs Eliza Golding a confectioner in Smith Street, Mrs Louisa Higgleton a butcher in the High Street and Mrs Caroline Murray, a midwife. Prittlewell (pre-dating Southend) has an ironmonger (Mrs Emma Barnard of

North Street); a couple of bakers and shopkeepers; a milk-seller (Mrs Phoebe Pledger of Leigh Road), and two pub landladies – Mrs Susannah Rutter at the Plough Inn and another at the Golden Lion in North Street. The Southchurch area (between Southend and Shoeburyness) features Miss Caroline Lloyd as the national school mistress; Mrs Marie Rawlins, milliner and dressmaker at Nursery Place; Mrs Katherine Wilks, tobacconist. Southend (specifically) lists seven schoolmistresses; a tobacconist; a 'mangling' business; drapers; fruiterer; hairdresser; laundress; stationers; haberdashers; a mantle-maker, and a wine merchant. Things were moving on as the century drew to a close.

The vast majority of women (into double figures) listed in Southend's Commercial Section at the end of the nineteenth century are shown as running apartments for holidays or residents, with a handful still running small private educational establishments. It was the growth of the holiday trade and the huge increase in visitors from London – thanks to the coming of the railway from London – that was responsible for so many women being able to make money from renting out a room or four. Southend became hugely popular with working class Londoners, especially those from the East End, as it was so close to the capital. Both day trippers and longer term holidaymakers, and their wallets, were welcomed with open arms. The town – which had grown from c. 2,500 residents in 1855 to over 62,000 in the 1880s – was no longer just the south end of Prittlewell parish.

Additional openings came as a result of the growth in tourism – waitresses, barmaids, tea-bar maids and cooks. Apart from women running retail outlets and public houses – such as the Britannia and the Falcon on the sea-front – they were applying for trade licences. Examples were Miss Cooper who operated the *camera obscura* on the pier in 1894 and Mrs Elizabeth Brown who was granted a licence to run a sherbet stand on the pier in April 1899. (The pier had been attracting tourists – and residents – since its opening in 1830 but had not really attracted much attention except as a landing jetty until the new iron pier opened in 1890, replacing horse-drawn trams with electric trains.) Mrs Ingram features regularly in the minutes of Southend's Licensing Committee, constantly renewing her licence to operate bathing machines on the beach, and, perhaps more bizzarely, Mrs Emma Barnard of North Street, Prittlewell, was granted (by the all-male Licensing Committee) a licence to keep petroleum in 1893.

In 1891 *Where To Buy At Southend* was published anonymously and, in part, acted as an early vehicle for complimentary reviews of businesses being run by local women. Mrs Purdy is described as having the 'happy knack of making everyone feel quite at home', at her boarding establishment on Westcliff Parade, Westward Ho (now a block of flats), although the manageress of this establishment was in trouble in May 1915 when she was fined for failing to obscure indoor lighting. Compliments were also paid to Mrs Edwards, who 'conducted' the Cigar Stores at 70 High Street and offered 'the anticipation of a pleasant and warm afternoon on the pier … armed with a newspaper or book and above all … a favourite pipe heavily charged with some of the excellent tobacco' obtained there. This latter establishment was 'well appointed in every respect' with quality products for 'the most exacting connoisseur or the most fastidious smoker alike being anticipated in its comprehensive selection', with all the necessary 'requisites [available] at the most reasonable cost', including 'cigar holders, pouches, match cases, cigar cases', for residents and visitors interested in 'extracting pleasure [from] the fragrant weed [who] cannot err in doing business with Mrs Edwards'.

Younger girls, or those struggling with other ways of earning a living, could find a whole range of ways of adding to the family income. For a 'small premium' they could become apprentice dress makers in the High Street – Mrs Beck advertised for two young ladies (pre-Sex Discrimination Act) in the *Southend Standard* in September 1873, so must have been doing well. Another option was to stand on a footpath and shout out: 'Clean lavatory here!' before the Corporation toilets were improved for visitors in the twentieth century. Rather similarly, the minutes of the Highways and Works Committee reported that there were seven applications for the job of caretaker and attendant at the female 'sanitary conveniences' being constructed on Royal Hill, offering 15*s* per week with hours of 8 a.m. – 11 p.m. for a seven-day week. No thoughts of exploitation or employment rights were on the agenda in 1896 and Miss Emma Vellensworth of North Road, who secured the appointment, was no doubt delighted. She was probably unaware of the existence of the Women's Industrial Council (from 1894) who promoted the interests of women at work (until the First World War).

The vast number of vacancies advertised for generally unskilled working-class young women at the end of the nineteenth century were in the domestic sphere. An 1898 copy of the *Southend Standard and Essex Weekly Advertiser* includes vacancies for 'general servants' in family settings, such as in the very smart Runwell Terrace or, for example, in the Cricketers Inn (still in situ in London Road). There are several positions advertised for local cooks, for 'clean and willing' or 'respectable' girls with undefined duties, but there were new opportunities creeping in – apprentice dressmakers, a girl to 'wrap' confectionery at a High Street address, or a 'young lady' to 'learn boot trade' in Nelson Terrace. Five years later, in the same publication, were openings for millinery apprentices while also continuing to list domestic vacancies with some variation, e.g., 'taking care of a baby five weeks old', or 'waiting entirely on an invalid', and some local history books mention the employment of nannies.

Unemployed women with limited education and skills were also tempted into prostitution; in 1890 there was a public sermon by Reverend Waller and Bishop Gregg revealing that prostitutes 'regularly congregated under the cliff' at Southend. There is also a reference (in a booklet about 'Old Rochford Hospital') to Union Lane, the location of Rochford workhouse, having a bit of a reputation, with 18-year-old Emily and 16-year-old Elizabeth being named as prostitutes working 'from a wooden shed' there in 1871. The Census for that year for the Female Lock Hospital and Asylum in Paddington lists Eliza Stibbard, a 17-year-old domestic servant from Southend, as one of its inmates; the Lock Hospitals had been introduced to 'cure' infected sex workers. There is also a report in the *Southend Standard and Essex Weekly Advertiser* (27 February 1908) of a local 'madam' – Kate Ridgwell – keeping 'a disorderly house' in Farringdon Place in 1908. She was employing teenage girls and taking at least £2 per week from each girl out of their earnings; she had been observed by local police officers and ended up in court, where she pleaded guilty and was fined £10 plus 11*s* 6*d* costs, with a two-month prison sentence if she defaulted.

More encouragingly, according to *The Chelmsford Chronicle* of 23 September 1904, from the end of October 1904, the Hockley Laundry (north of Southend) would provide home and work for able-bodied middle-aged women from Rochford Workhouse, enabling them to put a 'few shillings together' before going out into the world. The laundry would also take mending orders for clothes, the scheme funded initially to the tune of £100 by Mrs Augusta Tawke, of whom more later.

There were some occasional surprises, especially where the middle classes were concerned. Matilda Sharpe-Chatfield died in 1873 at the age of 62 and was buried in St John's churchyard; her tombstone states that she had been the Lady Superintendent of the Home for Disengaged Governesses for eleven years. This establishment was in Harley Street, London, intended as a place of residence for governesses between engagements, offering financial aid, an employment register, and an asylum for 'aged governesses'. The root cause of hardship for governesses was recorded as inadequate education! Matilda presumably commuted to London using the newly established railway line from Southend Central station.

Before the advent of the First World War, the latest Factory and Workshop Act (1901) required that, among other things, lists of outworkers were supplied by employers, mainly in the garment-making industry. It seems that in 1908, Mrs Wilson of 107 Hamlet Court Road did not furnish the council with this list, in contravention of the Act, as per the council's minutes. Whether she was the only one, and whether she was fined or otherwise 'punished' does not seem to be documented. Such acts were introduced over the years to protect, in particular, the employment of females and children. Working conditions were also monitored by the town's Health Committee, as recorded in council minutes, as when in May 1895 Mr F. Ramuz was ordered to make alterations to one of his properties, a building in the High Street being used as a workshop occupied by Miss Newberry (a dressmaker with six assistants). This property had insufficient sanitary conveniences, i.e., no running water – although it seems that this order was followed by the premises being vacated rather than improved!

Self employed women may have found life a little easier, with Mrs Beaumont on the pier taking on a tenancy to practice the then fashionable practice of phrenology, and Mrs Sears offering refreshments at the promenade level, paying £25 and £38 p.a. respectively in 1909. A year later, Mrs Alice Dawkins of Avenue Road in Westcliff was granted permission for ten bathing machines west of the pier at £1 per machine per season – such machines continuing in use well past the Victorian era. When Madam Vera Mervyn applied to the Pier Committee in 1912 for permission to occupy a Pier Hill building for clairvoyance and psychometry, this seems to have been a step too far and was declined, as was Mrs Holmes who had the idea of a day nursery for the children of 'excursionists', which was rejected on the grounds of the 'congested state of the foreshore' during the Summer. However, the continued growth in tourism meant that donkey rides increased in popularity and more licences for women to ply their donkeys for hire were granted, each woman restricted to a particular stretch of the seafront by the Highways and Works Committee. Even nurses – especially those with maternity experience – were advertising privately in the *Southend Standard and Essex Weekly Advertiser* in 1910, five of them in the 20 October issue alone.

Although the Rochford Board of Guardians mainly concerned itself with all things related to the Rochford workhouse, there was a digression into the subject of the employment of barmaids at their meeting in December 1903. The twenty-six-strong board – which included two women – had received a warning from the memorialists, a Christian religion, stressing that 'much evil' resulted from employing young girls in public houses, and the discussion was reported in the *Southend Standard*.

> They did not desire to interfere with women already in such employment, but asked that no further girls should be employed in such service. Girls so employed could not get work when youth was passed. The calling rapidly used up their strength and left them stranded at middle age. Barmaids of thirty were rare. It was a sad fact known to rescue workers that many fallen women had been barmaids. By a certain class of customers they were habitually subjected to insult which could not be described in that memorial. There was no country in the world where the employment of girls in bars was so common as in England. It was hoped that by discountenancing and discouraging the employment of barmaids to help to preserve modesty, strength, and womanliness and the future womanhood of the land. Colonel Lamb proposed that they support the memorial and the proposal was carried, Mr J. Tabor, J.P., being the only dissentient.

The Southend Council Minutes give revealing insights into the involvement of local women, some struggling, some stressed. The Health Committee of September 1906 for instance refers to the nursing staff at the Victoria Hospital (then in Warrior Square) being overworked – suggesting that nothing changes as the years go by. The Highways and Works Committee, at an earlier meeting, renewed the licence of the tenant of the Happy Valley Band Stand – a Mrs Newman. The Public Library Committee, to quote other 1906 examples, mention the new public library in Victoria Avenue appointing four female assistants and three junior assistants at between 5*s* and 17*s* 6*d* per week, dependent upon age and experience, with a Miss Pocklington deciding to sell the stock of her circulating library in Nelson Street onto the new library for £8 (it is now Southend

Central Museum). For those with a different cultural interest, there were vacancies in 1910 for usherettes at the Empire Palace in Leigh-on-Sea Broadway, which involved wearing black frocks and white aprons, one of their duties being to spray the auditorium from time to time with Jeyes Fluid, possibly because of the fisherfolk among its visitors.

Following the 1870 Education Act, the number of female teachers providing elementary education nationally increased by 800 per cent between 1873 and 1914. Before that, women looking to become schoolmistresses would be helped by family connections. The 1866 Post Office Directory, for example, shows the national and endowed schools in Southend employing, among others, a Mrs Josefin Jarvis as mistress (alongside the master, Richard Jarvis) and Miss Eliza Bigsby as mistress at Prittlewell, with George Bigsby as master. Locally, by the beginning of the twentieth century, the number of opportunities within the teaching profession escalated as the number of schools increased (see Chapter One). It was becoming the profession of choice for educated young women, especially those of the middle classes – in fact, there were fifty-three applications for the headmistress-ship of Leigh Road Junior Mixed School in December 1904.

Many local schools remained open during the First World War, offering some security of employment for its female teachers. It was not until long after this war – and after women had secured the vote – that the idea of equality with male teachers became an issue. The National Union of Women Teachers had their conference in Southend at the end of 1931 and carried a resolution 'demanding' equal pay for male and female teachers. A past president of the union (Miss Burls) said that they were sometimes 'told that women had not as good health as men. But women had given up migraines and vapours for athletics, running, and swimming. They demanded equal pay for equal work, because they did the same job. They wanted to be paid as workers, and not as women.'

The First World War did not initially make much of a dent in the type of work available to women locally, women who even more than ever needed to earn a living while their menfolk were in the forces. There were well over 200 vacancies for domestic workers advertised in the *Southend on Sea Observer* of 3 February 1915: housemaids, between maids, kitchen maids, scullery maids, nursemaids, parlourmaids, door housemaids (all of these for girls over the age of 14), plus vacancies for older women such as cooks and housekeepers. There was a shortage of clerical staff in the town generally as the war advanced, and Clark's College appealed for 150,000 girls to train to replace them – a little ambitious. The growth in the use of the typewriter was reflected in the new opportunities open to women locally and nationally. Regular advertisements for typists, and shorthand-typists, started appearing in the *Southend Standard and Essex Weekly Advertiser* from 1910.

The general British male reluctance for women to work at all was slowly relaxing, an idea reinforced by the Chair of the Women's Imperial Health Association who spoke at a meeting in Shoeburyness in August 1915 (reported in the *Southend and Westcliff Graphic*). She referred to women doing 'splendid work in the Red Cross, managing canteens for soldiers, working in munitions or driving motor ambulances', but was still aware that the 'greatest national service' women could offer was to 'put in the forefront the claims of the rising generation', i.e. parenting. Voluntary wartime 'work' was regarded rather differently, though again, there were mixed feelings. While the members of the Southend Needlework Guild were meeting regularly at Clarence Hall to do 'splendid work' making clothing and sandbags for wartime use (to quote the *Southend and Westcliff Graphic*) the *Woman's Dreadnought* made an appeal to wealthy women 'not to start sewing … while women who have earned their bread by such tasks are left to starve'.

Women, did, however, begin to apply for rather different working roles as the shortage of men presented new opportunities. Fifty women applied for jobs in the local electricity works in London Road when it was partly converted into a munitions factory to produce shells in 1915, with the *Southend and Westcliff Graphic* referring to officers' wives joining the 'great body of munition workers' setting an example which 'cannot fail to have a helpful effect on their fellow workers'. The nearest large munitions factory was at the Kynoch factory in Corringham, but at least 130 Southend women commuted to and from this factory for what was a dangerous job with no regard for Health and Safety. Among the c. 5,000 female employees were London prostitutes who'd had the choice of prison or working with explosives. Southend's Catherine Mackintosh was one of those working at the Kynoch Munitions factory at Corringham from 1915, earning 4½*d* per hour. She stayed in accommodation provided by Kynoch at Corringham during the week, using the Corringham Light Railway to commute, and was pictured wearing fireproof khaki overalls and grit-free overshoes which would not produce sparks from the floor. The factory made cordite, guncotton, gun powder and cartridges, and was the site of several nasty accidents, with one woman losing an arm and others badly injured.

In May 1915 seventy local women applied for jobs on the buses and trams and several were employed as conductors, but, again, the existing male employees refused to work with them. These men were actually dismissed but, according to council minutes, were reinstated after expressing their regret. When female supervisors were suggested on the trams in April 1917, this was regarded as a step too far, and male employees went on strike. A meeting of the National Federation of Discharged Sailors and Soldiers in December 1917 at the Masonic Hall in the High Street passed a resolution protesting about the seven lady tram drivers employed when 'discharged men were in want of employment'. How much effect this resolution had goes unrecorded. The situation had been rather different at the start of the war, when Leigh-born Annie Overton became the first female tram driver in Britain at the age of 17; she had been welcomed as 'one of the boys', and was apparently nicknamed 'Jimmy' so she would feel at home!

A reminder that the suffragette cause had been put on hold during the sar (see Chapter Six) came with the speech by Alderman Burrows at Southend High School for Girls

Certificate Giving Ceremony in 1917. He is quoted in *The Girls of Southend High School* as 'deploring' the violence 'associated with the agitation among women before the war', but 'gratefully recognised that directly the war broke out, they readily came forward to help their country. In increasing numbers from day to day women had been called upon to take the places of men and had done so with willingness and success.' Women were learning additional skills thanks to the loss of male workers – the Women's Legion, for example, trained thousands of women to drive and maintain motor vehicles.

Other new opportunities included producing khaki tents for the troops at Turnnidge Sailmakers in Leigh-on-Sea. Young girls who could handle a bicycle were also recruited to replace telegraph boys at the Post Office, and were provided with smart blue uniforms and straw hats, with the first local postwoman in situ in Leigh in 1916. Women and children replaced young men running milk carts through the streets dispensing the milk to the customers of Howard's Dairies. Some joined the newly founded Land Army, which provided them with a free basic uniform (which they could upgrade with leather boots from Harrods if they were so inclined!), progressing from the impractical nature of the skirt to the more practical option of breeches, avoiding showing their ankles. There were now plenty of female staff in local shops, most of which stayed open during the war years. It does appear, however, that the Hon. Sec. of the Southend and District Grocers' Association was not particularly fond of employing women in the grocery businesses, because they were only satisfactory 'up to a point', and not when 'left in charge' (quoted in the *Essex Newsman* of 29 June 1918). He felt it was 'hard to get women assistants at all, as women now chose employment which involved less labour and less hours'. Nevertheless, from cleaning trains or fish-curing to tea-bar maid, waitress or dressmaker, local working-class women now had a choice, albeit limited.

The Women's Auxiliary Force had branches in Southend and Westcliff by 1914, and some of these were depicted in the *Southend and Westcliff Graphic* (11 September) as crack-shots and expert signallers. The Women's Emergency Corps was formed in Southend in August 1914 'to utilise women in less obvious ways', according to the *Southend and Westcliff Graphic*. This evolved into the Women's Volunteer Reserve set up locally to fundraise, but also to work on signalling, dispatch riding on motor cycles or bicycles, care of horses etc – although an expensive £2 uniform was a bit of a deterrent to some joining.

It has been possible to track down just a handful of references to specific local women joining the Women's Army Auxiliary Corps which employed women at home and overseas from 1916 as part of the British Army but kept them away from the trenches, with their duties mainly confined to cooking, sewing and first aid. These are:

- Eileen Sinclair, 19, born in Southend, who was sent to the London Command Depot Laundry in May 1918, first as a laundress, and later a waitress. She was moved to St Albans in 1919 after being fined for refusing to obey an order, and moved another couple of times the same year – to Bostall Heath (Abbey Wood, South London) and Risborough Barracks at Folkestone before leaving at the end of 1919 and returning to family in Kent. Archived references for her show that she was 'fairly' industrious, and her medical notes include her height (5ft 6in) and chest measurement (34½in).
- Matilda Lester, 20, from Bell House, Eastwood Brickfields, Shoeburyness, 5ft 1in and with a chest measurement of 33½in (described as 'robust'), who signed up in June 1918 for domestic duties. She worked at the Connaught Club in Seymour Street London as well as also doing a stint at Bostall Heath in Abbey Wood and at the School of Military Engineering at Chatham. Her references describe her as hard-working, clean and honest but it seems she did not get to serve in France as per her application form.
- Annie Amoss, born to a farm labourer in Shoeburyness, joined up in July 1917 at the age of 30, by which time she was working in up-market Kensington as a cook. Her references describe her as very willing and hard-working, with medical details as 5ft ½in and 33in chest. She also

applied to work in France but seems to have got no further than the Connaught Club and Aldershot; somewhere along the way she married, because the paperwork for her departure in December 1918 lists her as Mrs Annie Lees.

- Emily Williams, from George Street, Shoeburyness, 19, joined in September 1918 (5ft 5in, chest 33½in), having been a domestic servant. In fact, one of her references is mono-syllabic with the comment 'she was simply my servant'. (No service record.)
- Kathleen Belcham from Bournemouth Park Road, Southend, age 20, offered her clerical experience in August 1918, but was discharged a year later as 'surplus to requirements'. (Again, no service record.)
- Lucy Johnson, born in Southend, 18 when she signed up in 1918, and having been a kitchen maid did quite well, as she served as a cook at the Connaught Club in London.
- Winifred Sharp, born in Southend, 30, an experienced waitress and kitchen maid when she joined up in 1918. Notes record her as 5ft 5in, 30½in chest, and 'slight'. By March 1919, she had met a Canadian soldier and applied for discharge so she could apply for a passport and marry. She also seems to have worked at the Connaught Club, which looks to have been a good location for husband-hunting.

While the National Archives were a fruitful source for army records, no corresponding information has been found relating to Southend women joining the Women's Royal Naval Reserve or the Women's Royal Air Force (from 1918).

Not only did post-war women relinquish their wartime roles to men, but also had additional duties of care for disabled husbands and fathers. Not all women gave up their jobs voluntarily – three women working for the council were dismissed in 1920 at the instigation of Alderman Meachen who had received a letter from the National Federation of Discharged and Demobilised Sailors and Solders calling attention to their dispensable employment. In fact, women who wanted to continue working after the First World War were considered unpatriotic, and a marriage bar in many professions (e.g. teaching, nursing and the civil service) was not dropped until after the Second World War. Some new openings were as a direct result of the war, however, with poor women living near Shoebury Garrison able to earn a little money by taking in washing for the soldiers, carried in a wheelbarrow, or by providing hot lunches in a basin covered with a cloth for those men working in local brickfields. Plus, as a result of the troops billeted there, trade was gradually boosted, and began to thrive with at least seven grocers, butchers, greengrocers, chemists, barbers, cobblers, tea rooms, and confectioners.

Women were generally expected to return to their domestic roles after the war, not just locally. The 1919 Restoration of Pre-War Practices Act meant that most women had to leave their jobs to make way for the men. Those that stayed could expect fifty per cent of the equivalent male salary. A lot of women, however, returned to a life of caring for injured family members, or widowhood. The plethora of such widows meant that women had to be more and more enterprising. In Leigh-on-Sea High Street, Kate Davies was just 35 when she was widowed in 1919, left to earn a living and bring up a young son. With a background as a housemaid before marriage and a housewife since 1902, she turned to organising charabanc outings, advertising 'Comfort and Safety First' – a veritable Thomas Cook. Then there was Annie Layzell of Tunbridge Road who crammed seventeen tenants into her six-room house (apparently rising to twenty-five during the summer!), taking full advantage of the housing shortage after the war. The Sex Disqualification Removal Act of 1919 helped some women, as it meant they could become lawyers or vets for example.

As the role of women began to evolve, nationally, and women slowly began to get the vote (some in 1918, the rest in 1928 – see Chapter Six), Southend spawned a few musical women. Muriel Gratten (born 1902) played the organ in the Theatre de Luxe cinema (her mother also a professional musician) something that attracted other women like Ena Baga. The Baga family had moved to Southend from London for their health in the early twentieth century, and Ena and her sisters were all professional organists who went on to entertain audiences between films once talkies came along, heralding new long-term careers for some. Freda Parry's family also moved to the Westcliff area for her health when she was just 6 in 1904, and she trained at the Metropolitan Academy of Music, setting up the Freda Parry Ladies Choir in 1924 which still exists. Mary Beaumont was a little less fortunate, as she had to pay for the pleasure of practising the organ at the Wesley Methodist Church in Leigh in the 1920s – at 6*d* a time. Another new opportunity was to teach dancing – a Miss Ella Willmer of Westcliff-on-Sea advertised her skills in the *Southend Standard and Essex Weekly Advertiser* of 3 December 1908. She offered lessons in 'Stage and Fancy Dancing' at 'moderate fees'. In the world of theatre, there was one regular music hall artiste at Southend Hippodrome in the early part of the twentieth century who had a higher profile public life as a militant suffragette: Kitty Marion, who also spoke out against the 'casting couch'. One woman, Mrs Eleanor Perry, became chair of the directors of the Warrior Square Picture Theatre in the 1920s, with another, Gertrude Mouillot, actually going as far as donating the Palace Theatre (Westcliff) to the town.

The largest employer in Southend in the 20s and 30s was E. K. Cole, the radio and plastics manufacturer, including a high percentage of women (2,000 in 1932). Women were mainly involved in assembly, winding and reeling, packing, soldering, with transformers taking shape 'under these dainty and dexterous fingers', to quote the *Southend Standard* of 25 August 1932. The female staff here were well looked after – there were hockey and netball teams, a band and a cabaret team to entertain staff, plus a ladies' physical training team and an athletics team which incorporated walking, cycling and the high jump.

A Women's Association for Mistresses and Maids was formed in 1924 together with a servants' registry office said to have found work for 500 girls (according to an unidentified press cutting in Southend's library.) The same source refers to queues of women forming whenever a job for a charwoman was advertised. There was also seasonal work between the wars for female cockle and shrimp packers. In 1928, the Mayor's Unemployment Bureau in Clarence Road was boasting a 'Women's Section' offering 'reliable charwomen, cooks, housemaids, daily helpers' at a month's notice, and appealing to local employers to offer work, even if temporary. There were also more opportunities in Leigh-on-Sea from this time as this too began to grow as a residential area attracting all kinds of retail outlets, with shops opening in Broadway West including a fruiterer's run by Marjorie Simkins, a confectioner's run by Edith Clark and a refreshment bar headed up by Mrs Fanny Coppitter.

But other careers started to materialise between the wars – Stella Read is believed to have been the first woman to join a motorcyclist patrol team, there was a Mrs Lamb serving as a probation officer, and a Margaret Clarke who became a popular photographer, moving from a studio in Leigh to other locations in central Southend in the 40s and 50s. Others took jobs on by default, such as Mrs Hewitt-Wilson, whose husband was one of the first photographers in Southend, when the High Street was a place you could go bird-watching. He died in 1860 leaving her with twelve children, so she carried on the business for thirty years and was the only photographer with a pass to Shoebury Garrison entitling her to take photographs of officers, personnel and visitors – including Princess Louise, the Prince Regent, the Duchess of Teck and Princess May of Teck. Similarly, Mrs Sawkins took over from her blacksmith husband in Shoeburyness following his death in 1929. The iron and wood hut on the beach had some extra customers in the form of famous boxers who used the forge's hammers as additional exercise after spending time at the gym at the Shoebury Hotel. Even the wife of a naval captain, a Mrs Townend living at Shoebury Hall in the 1930s, found she was short of money for her family, so began using the land attached to her home to breed cocker spaniels, raise chickens and provide farmhouse teas, a business which developed into offering accommodation in the form of a tented camping site with straw provided for the palliases (see *The Shoebury Story*).

There was a female almoner at the old Victoria Hospital (i.e. before 1932), and female operating department assistants at the new hospital by 1934, but no female doctors for another two years, their appointment having been declared 'unsuitable' up to this point as per council minutes. Female consultant obstetricians were appointed in the 1940s, improving infant mortality, almost to the point of non-existence by 1951. The first women porters appeared in 1944, and were paid ninety per cent of the male rate for their first year, then equal pay for equal work – an interesting statistic (from *The Old Rochford Hospital*). Nurses had to follow some strict rules between the wars when training, revealed in an anonymous nurse's notebook in the Essex Record Office, assumed to be from the 1930s. These are some of her jottings:

- hair needed to be 'neatly dressed and parted in the middle with no fancy pins'
- visitors must be treated with 'courtesy at all times, even if trying'
- 'no meal to be missed without permission'
- 'no talking shop at mealtimes'
- wait until 'after Grace' before leaving the dining room
- 'no laughing in corridors'
- 'no arguing'
- 'lights out 10.30 p.m.'
- 'beds stripped before 6.35 a.m. and re-made before 10 a.m.'

As for women librarians, they were not yet rated very highly, as confirmed by Alderman Miles, J.P., who held (in the *Thameside Mail* of 29 July 1926) that their salaries should not be increased as suggested in a council meeting, because the job made 'no great demand on physical energy or intelligence'. While other councillors supported an increase, the motion was lost. A year later, when planning a new library for adjacent Leigh-on-Sea, they were unable to obtain 'girls with the qualifications laid down by the Council … as authorized at the last meeting', so that vacancies had been filled temporarily with 'girls without qualifications …' (*Southend Standard* 22 September 1927). On the subject of books, incidentally, one-time-famous local author Warwick Deeping seems to have inherited his skill for writing from his mother Marianne, but she had failed to get her writing published at the end of the nineteenth and early twentieth century – possibly because she was a woman, though there is no proof of this.

Interestingly, a number of women were patrolling (not quite policing!) local parks and pleasure grounds before the 20s, ostensibly to 'prevent mischief' (the *Chelmsford Chronicle* 21 November 1924 *et al*). These Women's Patrols were finding shelter for the homeless, doling out advice, even finding foster mothers or helping with the disciplining of children. The patrols were reported as having done 'extremely good and important work' especially with regard to summer visitors who found themselves stranded, the local Medical Officer referring to the 'serious menace' of 'the flapper'! The patrols were disbanded in 1933 even though their role had expanded to include an element of what was then described as 'delicate' welfare work, and although they were even paying fares to London for those stranded; Miss Absalom of Alexandra Street was singled out in appreciation of her work as Patrol Leader.

Female unemployment in the 1930s increased – from 1,326 in 1937 to 2,266 in 1939 (according to Donald Glennie in *Our Town*). And women were a long way behind the men when it came to wages in the 30s – female agricultural workers in Southend, for instance, were paid 10*d* to 1*s* per day, with men paid approximately double (same source). According to the *Southend Standard,* there was a proposal by Essex (not Southend) County Council in May 1935 to pay men and women equal pay if they were doing the same work, but this was not carried. Not only that, there were still female workers as young as 13 recorded in 1933 when one girl was paid 2*s* 6*d* for twenty hours work over the weekend peeling potatoes and washing dishes in a local restaurant (see *Seaside Entrepreneurs*). Not surprisingly, there were many complaints about working conditions – especially for women – in the catering industry prior to the Second World War, where a working week could be ninety-six hours in the summer season. There was also a claim in *The Southend Story* that by the 1930s, when 3,000 Southenders were out of work during the great depression, the reluctance of local girls to work in local factories made matters worse, their reasoning said to be because they did not like being referred to as 'factory hands'!

By the beginning of the Second World War, women were making real progress in the work place – it was no longer a rarity for a woman to join the army, navy, or even the air force. In fact, so many women enrolled in the local branch of the Women's Army Auxiliary Corps (WAAF) that a senior section officer was brought in to take charge – Pam Barton, once famous as a championship golfer. [In 1943, she took part in a golf match at Belfairs Park in Leigh-on-Sea, a few days before being killed in action.] Female volunteers were also welcomed with open arms – as ambulance drivers, messengers, air raid wardens or nursing auxiliaries; and the local WVS was formed in July 1939 with 1,650 Southend volunteers. An appeal was printed in the *Southend Standard* of 27 July 1939 for even more women to drive ambulances, act as messengers or air raid wardens, first aiders, nursing auxiliaries and blood donors. Women were also needed to help out as fire-watchers or as 'House Mothers' who cycled up and down local roads during an air raid to contact elderly or sick neighbours who might need help.

The move away from the stereotype of the female workforce was illustrated by a story in the *Daily Mirror* of 14 March 1939, giving an account of Miss Pottle's business in Beaufort Street, Southchurch, where she bred mice for research. The pre-war period was also a time for women to start to be involved in local organisations which had previously been the prerogative of the men. The Shoeburyness branch of the Royal Artillery Association, for example, formed a Ladies Guild before the Second World War, and eventually opened membership to the wives and widows of ex-gunners and to ex-ATS who had served with the gunners, even though there was no suitable accommodation until 1948 at a new drill hall. Winston Churchill's wife lent a hand during the 1940s by opening a centre for ATS women in Wakering Road as a quiet haven away from the male environment, which also included welcome laundry facilities.

Women in Southend, who for many reasons remained in the town, had even more important roles to play than in the First World War. When incendiary bombs were dropped on the town in 1941, the *Southend Standard* described local womenfolk as the 'Bucket and Spade Brigade' because they rushed from home with spades and pails to minimise the damage. The Women's Auxiliary Force was boosted locally in 1941 when Southend became under-policed due to the male shortage, but extra suitable accommodation was found for the women in the Alexandra Street Police Station. Similarly, the Women's Home Defence (a sort of female Home Guard) was up and running in the area by 1942. The *Essex Chronicle* quotes MP Dr Edith Summerskill's speech at a Southend meeting on 25 November when she said that 'if invasion came, a woman's place was not under the table, not behind the door, or in a strong man's arms – he would have the job of repelling the invader – she must put herself to the maximum use … some 30,000 women were first class shots.' While the quote negating the female role in 'repelling the invader' might be rather contentious, she otherwise reminded her audience of the changing roles of women, locally and nationally, and she became well known as an advocate of equal pay for men and women.

The women's branch of the British Army (the Auxiliary Territorial Service) was a popular choice for Southend women – there were literally hundreds displaying their skills at Shoebury Garrison during a visit by the Princess Royal in October 1943. Incidentally, the first ATS Experimental Assistants in Gunnery had arrived at the Garrison in 1940, and one of their Corporals (Gerry Kelly), who had been put on a charge for being inappropriately dressed (in battledress rather than navy skirt and pullover), was instrumental in finally introducing this more practical uniform for the EAG women. The local WAAF had similar strong support.

In September, 1941, the *Southend-on-Sea and County Pictorial* published an appeal to the 'Women of Southend' in an attempt to recruit even more women for the ATS and for 'war work in the great Arms Factories'. Their appeal was direct:

'Our War Work Week is your chance to show the world that the women of Southend are doing their utmost for Victory, and the freedom and peace it will bring to us and our children.'

Apart from the services, there were other unique ways of contributing to the war effort. Thames Naval Control (who had taken over part of Royal Terrace) employed clerical officers on confidential duties who had to work in locked, secret rooms, and sign the Official Secrets Act. These women had access to the confidential plans for the D-Day landings, and dealt with details of the beach landings and routings. The Swallow Raincoat Company took over part of the Kursaal to make raincoats for the National Fire Service as well as waterproof clothing for the forces, employing over 100 women, with some of the female employees slipping notes 'of encouragement' into the pockets of garments intended for the army. Some local women were making camouflage nets (messy, fiddly work), some had white collar work at the ARP Control centre in Victoria Avenue, other outdoorsy types joined the Land Army. Although E.K. Cole's factory (EKCO) evacuated many of its staff and much of its production away from Southend for the duration of the war, some remained, working on intercoms for tank crews, and on receivers and wiring looms for Lancaster bombers. The emphasis had moved away from domestic radios and televisions, with Bakelite now being used for plastic practice bombs, and valves replacing lamps.

October 1944 saw the inaugural meeting of the Southend branch of the National Association of Local Government Officers (NALGO), with seven women on its sub-committee, one from each council department in which women were employed. Women were slow to join the union, 62 of 600 joining in 1944, increasing to 97 by March 1945. The minutes of their meetings serve to reinforce how many departments were being effectively infiltrated by women – Transport, Borough Engineers, Rates, Machine Room – although, sadly perhaps, some of these were only temporary positions until men returned from the services. After the war (1949), the union lobbied local MPs to push for equal pay, and, in Southend's case, Sir Henry 'Chips' Channon said he would 'do all he could'. The *Southend Standard* reported in February 1950 that the Southend Professional and Business Women's Club had sent two questions to three local MPs (i.e. to the three parties: Tory, Labour, Liberal). Question One: Will the party continue to press for equal pay? Answer from all: Yes. Question Two: Will the party admit peeresses to the House of Lords? Answer from all (more evasive): Up to the House to decide, but in favour. It would be two more decades before there was any real progress, nationally and locally, of course.

It was as early as May 1947 that the newly formed Southend Branch of the Union of Shop, Distributive and Allied Workers opened a campaign for a £5 minimum wage for a five-day working week of forty hours. (As the Royal Commission on Equal Pay in 1946 had concluded tentatively that women in teaching and certain grades of the civil service 'might' benefit from equal pay, the assumption is that USDAW's eventually successful campaign included both sexes.) In the same year, Southend finally had two policewomen in situ, the police force having had some difficulty in recruiting women other than for its clerical vacancies in Alexandra Street and its other local stations in Leigh, Westcliff and Shoebury. There had been an attempt to recruit policewomen a few years earlier, but although a number of women applied, they failed to reappear after hearing the conditions of service! This was also the period when, for the first time, there was a shortage of domestic labour in the town.

In 1948, as a result of teacher shortages following the war, an emergency training scheme was initiated. At least one local woman, Gladys Mude, took advantage of this and took part in a one-year crash course at Bedford following her interview. She wanted a change from her work at E.K. Cole and this proved a good move for her, as she could choose her specialisation. She chose singing and violin, securing a two-year probationary role at West Leigh Schools (and later winning a music scholarship to London's Guildhall).

Nationally, the post-war benefit system was firmly based on the notion that society was organised into family units with a male breadwinner. Married women, therefore, were not entitled to benefits on the assumption that they were dependants of the male head of household, conveniently overlooking how important women's labour was to the economy. State day nurseries which had been opened to meet the need of women workers during the war closed, making it even more difficult for working-class women to earn a much-needed income. The TUC had decided in 1949 (following the Beveridge Report, so influential in the founding of the welfare state) that equal pay was 'inappropriate at the present time' because of 'the continuing need for counter inflationary policies', indicating a continuance of women's oppression in the workplace, nationally and locally. This is perhaps demonstrated by usherette Joan Davis, dismissed from her £2 per week job at the Coliseum Cinema in Southend in June 1947 because of union activity. It fell to the middle-class women, as with suffrage, to fight again for their working sisters. Women would start 1950 with plenty more to fight for.

CHAPTER THREE

Women at Home

It will come as no surprise that home lives are affected by class and money, in Southend as anywhere else. While the first social housing in the UK was in the East End of London at the end of the nineteenth century, it took some years for this to be part of Southend's town planning. A committee for the Housing of the Working Classes was formed locally in 1899. This was the year when, in November, the *Southend Standard* reported on a meeting on the subject at the Co-Operative Assembly Room in Southchurch Road, chaired by Alderman Burrows. The meeting revealed a 'housing famine' in the town with the need for 'model' housing for the working classes. In the meantime, poorer families lived in over-crowded rented properties in different parts of the town, with limited sanitation, while those with very different incomes, inherited or earned, owned several large properties and extensive swathes of land. Alderman Thompson pointed out, graphically, that:

> death came in a slum not in a moment by a shot, but slowly through the deadly cancer, insidious consumption, one or other form of zymotic disease – lingering, dragging on month after month with no glory in it, no pension, no widow and orphan fund and no benefit to anyone other than the owner of that slum.

Women married to the troops based at Shoebury Garrison had the benefit of married quarters from 1869, albeit of a very basic construction known as 'black huts', whose roofs lifted when there were particularly loud experimental explosions in the vicinity. More married quarters were built in 1876, with Birdcage Quarters built in 1899, so-called because of the railings on their front balconies. This location was also handy for the poor to top up their fuel supply with an occasional lump of coal dropped from barrows en route from the barges. The military atmosphere of this area, incidentally, prevented the three unmarried Knapping sisters, Margaret, Edith and Gertrude (they inherited money from their father, who was behind the profitable local brickfields), from turning the East Beach frontage into their idea of a high-class holiday area, as did the cold winds prevailing.

By July 1900, a committee meeting revealed that only twenty purpose built homes had been provided for Southend residents, and overcrowding was a big problem. Data was produced that detailed dwellings with as many as twelve people living in four rooms, this was also linked to infant mortality rates and the spread of disease. Plans were proposed for a further sixty semi-detached houses for poorer families east of Sutton Road, so slow progress was being made. From 1870, orphaned or destitute girls dependent on charity were taken in by St Mary's orphanage in Milton Road, run by the Sisters of Notre Dame. From 1876 however, they might have ended up in Dr Barnardo's Village Home for Girls in Barkingside, a few miles to the west. It was certainly a better option than the workhouse; at least one Leigh girl was an inmate in 1901, and is recorded as learning laundry skills.

With the introduction of a regular train route to London in 1856, the area developed as a holiday resort and more rooms for visitors were needed; the situation was exacerbated by the introduction of Bank Holidays in 1871. More than just rooms were required, additionally, as Southend developed as a commuter town, with a population of 53,000 by 1908 according to the town council (double the figure in the *ABC Railway Guide*). When Mrs Leeman was fined £1 plus 4*s* costs in 1912 for failing to provide privy accommodation for the occupiers of a van used for human habitation on the Coleman Estate (per

Southend Health Committee Minutes), this is indicative of the shortage of accommodation available.

At an earlier meeting (1901) of the Unitarian Social Union, Councillor Doody gave a talk on Housing for the Poor. He was grateful for the support of the government, which empowered 'local bodies to borrow money for securing sites, and erecting workmen's dwellings'. He then drew a picture of the

> disabilities under which the poor live in congested districts, where in a lodging of one or two rooms the jostling of birth and death … take place. The poor have in many instances scarcely room to live, what wonder that they are not so cleanly in their habits or refined in their moral tone as their more fortunate fellow creatures, who can afford better homes and have larger space in which to move about … it is greatly to the credit of those brought up under adverse circumstances if they can cultivate the white flower of a blameless life, but it is in the interest of morality, and therefore, of the community, to give greater facilities to working people to live clean, healthy, self-respecting lives.

Councillor Doody showed that it was vital to expand housing in a way that was necessary, practical and 'not likely to entail any additional burden on the rate-payers'. He also pointed out that a much 'higher proportion of a wage earner's salary was eaten by rent than ought to be the case', with 'surroundings … of an insanitary nature … with insufficient space for the free passage of air', and with landlords 'able to command a much higher rent than their actual outlay justified'. He didn't mention the local workhouse at Rochford dating from 1837 which continued to take desperate inmates until its various buildings, in the 1920s, became an infirmary, nurses' home and home for the 'feeble-minded' – with much of it demolished after the Second World War.

Diaries, letters, newspaper items and even oral histories relating to the home lives of working-class women in the town before the First World War are limited for a variety of reasons, but the mind-set is illustrated by such newspaper items as that of 21 November 1873 in the *Southend Standard.* This referred to the wife of Samuel Sullings of Rochford, a sawyer (saw mills were more common then than now, of course) who was in court in answer to a summons charging her husband with being 'drunk at Rochford on the 24th ult [of last month]'. She stated that she had not told her husband about the summons as he 'had just got work and it would be a pity for him to leave'. *He* was fined 1*s* and costs which *she* paid. There were also instances (see Chapter Two) of women in the workplace being protected, and of the start of organisations which helped poorer women. There was a local Robin Society based at Avenue Baptist Church, which offered free teas annually to the poorest local children and dispensed hot meals for the unemployed at Clarence Road. The first local Women's Institute was formed in 1915 to encourage women to grow and preserve food at a time of shortages, and the Southend Shelter for Girls and the Girls' Friendly Society were both doing what they could for local women in financial difficulties. The latter organisations continued with their work for many decades. The Girls' Friendly Society in Milton Road, established in Prittlewell in 1884, ran a busy hostel after the First World War, and was still offering lonely girls and women the opportunity to join their hostel's Christmas festivities in 1935.

The Reverend Dormer Pierce, spoke in praise of the work of what he called 'The Rescue and Preventive Home and Girls' Shelter' when in Westcliff, at a meeting in November 1913 attended by Lady Gwendolen Guinness. He said that Westcliff had 'set an example of family life which everybody would like to see spread all over the town [as] there were places of business in Southend where it was impossible for a young girl to live in purity'. St Monica's Home, the organisation behind the Southend Girls' Shelter, was praised again in 1925 by the Bishop of Chelmsford when he attended their annual meeting – he was in favour of preventing girls from 'frumping themselves with painted faces and pencilled eyebrows' in a desire to imitate the girls of Hyde Park and Piccadilly, the kind of life that 'led to ruin'. In 1929, 158 girls and five babies had been cared for at St Monica's, as reported in the *Chelmsford Chronicle* of 29 November. The Shelter closed its York Road base in 1940 when many women and children were evacuated, but reopened in 1941 acting primarily as a remand home for girls, continuing after the war to work mainly with unmarried mothers. The Superintendent of St Monica's spoke out in June 1950, suggesting that more sex instruction from parents was needed in order to prevent 'the problem of unmarried mothers' – she was speaking to another local organisation: the Southend Professional and Business Women's Club.

Before women had the vote, before the First World War, there were instances of local women leading less domestic lives and taking off into the unknown. The February 1913 magazine of the Avenue Baptist Church (in Westcliff) refers to Miss Lappage sailing for Canada and Miss Campkin sailing for Ceylon (to be married). The church's October meeting approved the transfer of Miss Gertrude and Miss Elsie Comber and Miss Gertie Winter to Canada, and in November Miss Daisy Hirst sailed from Tilbury to be married in Sydney. The same year saw 22-year-old Ada Ward (who was apparently a servant in Prittlewell) emigrating to Canada aboard the steamship *Andania,* where she married in 1914. In 1913, the majority of the Cohen family of Elmer Road, emigrated to New York. (Sarah Cohen had achieved some local fame around 1890, fundraising for the Boer War, and in being the bride at the first Jewish wedding in the town in 1907.) Mr and Mrs Cohen and their daughters Jennie, Beatrice, May and Violet arrived on the steamship *St Paul* around 10 a.m. on 10 January 1913. Their arrival was reported in a New York paper because of their status; they had purchased an apartment in the Bronx, and were met at the pier by a committee of masons. There are also records of an Agnes Bullworthy, aged 20, from nearby Thundersley, leaving for Canada with her father in 1914 to set up a home and bring the rest of the family over at a later date – whether war prevented these plans from coming to full fruition has proved elusive. There is one other reference, however, in *A Momentous*

Century, to the wife of the Reverend Parrinder who went, with her husband, to the French Ivory Coast as a missionary in 1930. At least two ex-pupils from Southend High School for Girls were involved in missionary work in Africa right through the 1940s – Nina Banks was in charge of the dispensary at the Church Missionary Society in Kampala, and Kathleen Brain with the Baptist Missionary Society in Zaire.

Emigration was not a twentieth-century phenomena, as in 1851, for instance, Mr and Mrs Kernot and their 6-year-old son emigrated from Rochford to Melbourne, and in June 1883 Mary Ann Burrell and her four children successfully applied to leave the workhouse to emigrate to Queensland. As it was cheaper to pay her £30 emigration allowance than continue to support the family indefinitely, the Guardians agreed. There are also records of two women from the local Absalom family emigrating from Prittlewell to Durban, South Africa, in 1863 – Annie and her sister Rose, the latter marrying in Durban and moving to New Zealand with her husband some years later.

Back home, the housing shortage was dealt with in a number of ways – as with the Attersley family who lived on board the 'Rosa John', a houseboat at Leigh Creek, from 1924–1935. Affordable accommodation post-war was in even shorter supply than before, and although the houseboat (along with others) was in very poor condition, it was refurbished to provide three bedrooms with double bunks, a kitchen, diner and WC to provide for six children. The children collected water from the tap by the cockle sheds after school, and the milkman and postman called at the houseboats, with produce available to purchase from the Theobalds' Farm nearby. This particular family even had a snooker table which could only be used when the windows were open to allow room for the cues! Other families managed to fit in a sewing machine or even a primitive workshop. There were eighteen houseboats, mostly housing large families, in 1921, increasing to over 200 by the 1930s. This rather eccentric lifestyle continued until 1950 when the landowners – the Salvation Army – sold the land to the council, and the boats were removed. (See *The Life and Times of the Houseboats of Leigh-on-Sea*.)

After the Second World War, and bearing in mind that Southend was affected by enemy bombing, homelessness became a problem, resulting in thirty homeless families marching on Butler's Camp in Shopland (just North of the town) in August, 1946, to commandeer the dwellings – ex-army accommodation. The local housing authority accepted the families as tenants and improved the facilities until more permanent accommodation was found.

At the same time, there was a local branch of the British Housewives League who were active in producing petitions and posters against rationing ('We Want More Meat'). Incidentally, there wasn't a choice of shops where you could exchange your ration coupons, as you had to 'register' with a specific shop, for example the Co-op. The big families that were so commonplace up to and including the 1940s actually did quite well – the more children, the more rations. However, once rationing began to be phased out, there were annual 'Ideal Home' exhibitions at the Kursaal, showing gadgets of every description to improve women's home life – and fashion shows for the less domestic. Apart from such innovations as Hartrite 'invisible' curlers, stocking ladder-menders, and perfume which came with a free horoscope, there were a number of stands featuring the latest cookers, and even washing machines and early televisions. There had, of course, been limited electricity (and sewerage for that matter) in some parts of the town since the end of the 1920s.

As early as 1861, Mrs Beeton was writing that 'a housewife's badly cooked dinners and untidy ways' were a fruitful source of family discontent. She does not mention a shortage of food, however, which was addressed at this time in Southend by a growing trend for keeping chickens where a backyard was available, and by growing herbs or a few vegetables if there was access to a couple of square metres of earth. When food-laden ships were destroyed by German action during the First World War, the reliance on imports began to rear its head, and much available land was then used to grow crops. The hockey pitch at Southend High School for Girls was used to grow vegetables, with the wartime headmistress spending part of her holidays

QUEEN ANNE'S COLLEGE FOR GIRLS.

WEST CLIFF PARADE, SOUTHEND-ON-SEA.

Principal :—MISS R. CHAPLIN,

Assisted by Resident and Visiting Mistresses and Masters.

QUEEN ANNE'S COLLEGE stands on the Parade, facing the sea, and is a large, commodious building, with large, airy bedrooms, bathrooms, and dining hall. The School House adjoins, and contains classrooms, music rooms, Kindergarten, etc.

Special attention is given to physical development, and classes for Swedish drill, gymnastics, and other exercises are held daily by a resident teacher. The present Mistress holds the Diploma of the Liverpool Gymnasium Training College. Bathing, swimming, and organised games are encouraged and supervised by the Mistress.

The pupils are prepared for the University Local Examinations, the Associated Board of the R.A.M. and R.C.M., Trinity College, and other examinations.

In the Preparatory department students are prepared and trained for the examinations of the Froebel Society by a Mistress holding the N.F.U. Higher Certificate.

Indian and Colonial girls are received for entire charge.

From *Paton's List of Schools* 1912

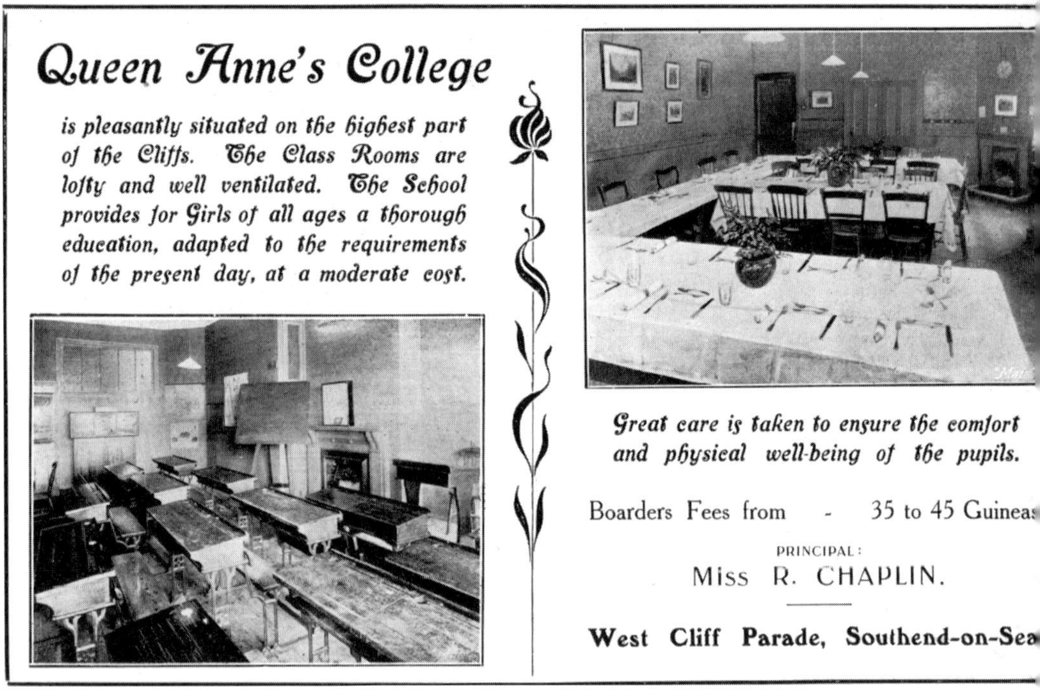

From *Mates Illustrated Guide to Southend-on-Sea* 1907

SOUTHEND'S FIRST LADY COUNCILLOR.
Miss Bannester, the principal of Alexandra College, who has been elected for the Westborough Ward. (Photo, A. L. Shepherd.)

From *Southend and Westcliff Graphic* 1910

Southend Technical School, Victoria Circus

Sports Day 1930

Jane Chennery's grave, **courtesy Elsa Hunter**

Seafront waitresses 1931, **courtesy** ***Southend Standard***

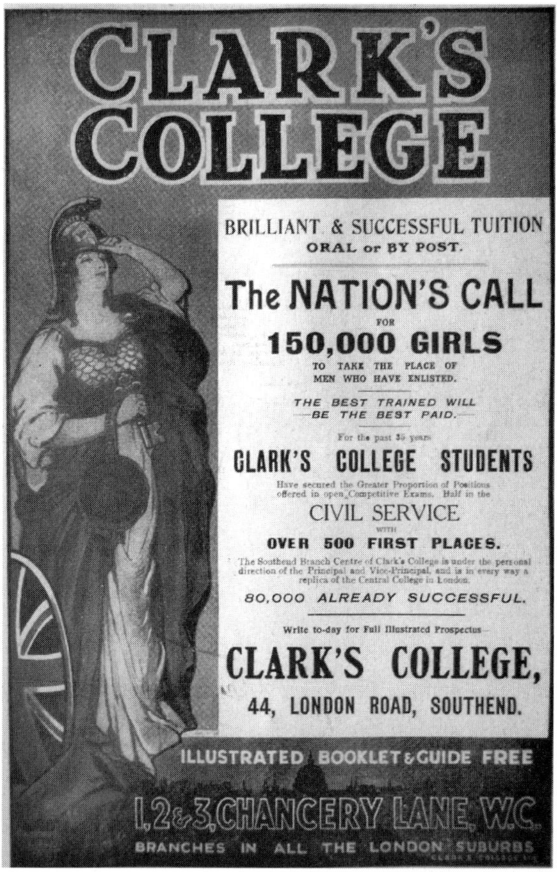

Right: From *Southend and Westcliff Graphic* 1916

Below: Reference for Emily Williams

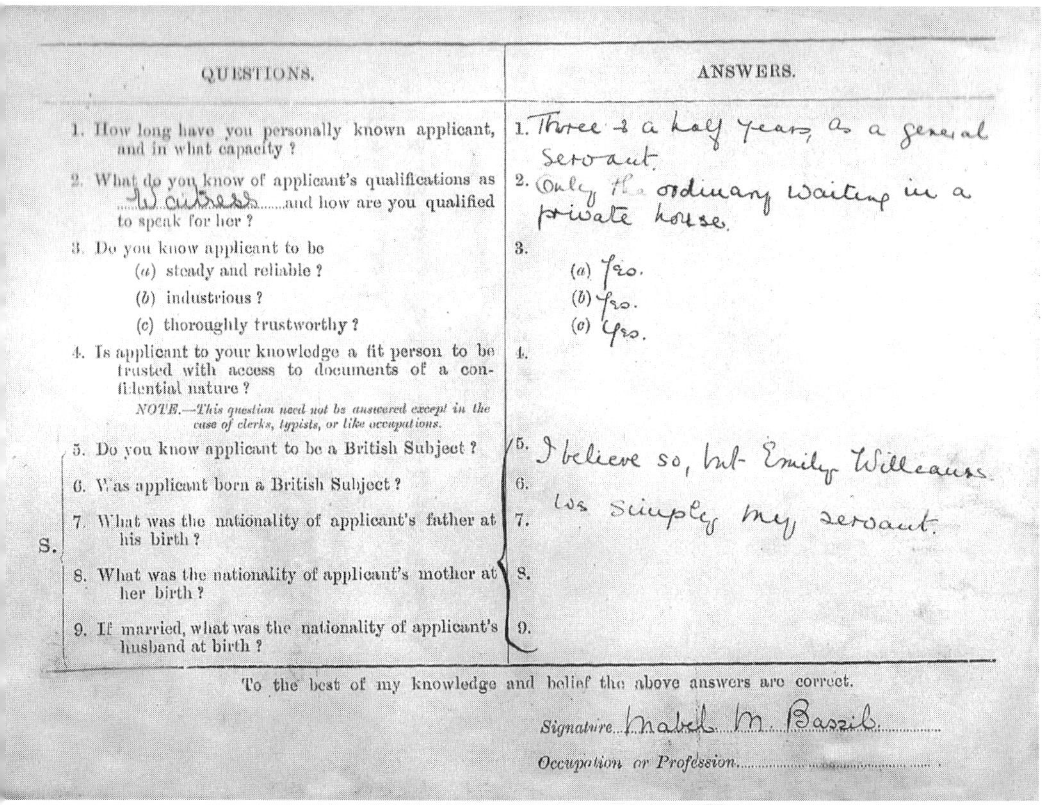

QUESTIONS.	ANSWERS.
1. How long have you personally known applicant, and in what capacity?	1. Three & a half years, as a general servant.
2. What do you know of applicant's qualifications as Waitress and how are you qualified to speak for her?	2. Only the ordinary waiting in a private house.
3. Do you know applicant to be	3.
(a) steady and reliable?	(a) Yes.
(b) industrious?	(b) Yes.
(c) thoroughly trustworthy?	(c) Yes.
4. Is applicant to your knowledge a fit person to be trusted with access to documents of a confidential nature? *NOTE.—This question need not be answered except in the case of clerks, typists, or like occupations.*	4.
S. 5. Do you know applicant to be a British Subject?	5. I believe so, but Emily Williams was simply my servant.
6. Was applicant born a British Subject?	6.
7. What was the nationality of applicant's father at his birth?	7.
8. What was the nationality of applicant's mother at her birth?	8.
9. If married, what was the nationality of applicant's husband at birth?	9.

To the best of my knowledge and belief the above answers are correct.

Signature Mabel M. Bassil

Occupation or Profession

Left: **Muriel Gratten, 1916, courtesy Graham Mee**

Below: Woman worker: 'I don't mind watering the hay-garden with the hose but you must shut up those dreadful wild, savage birds.'

Miss Tawke, of Hockley, stated at a meeting at Southend on the subject of farm work for women that one lady had written to say that she could not continue the work as there was a loose horse in the field, and another objected to the proximity of a calf! From *Southend and Westcliff Graphic* 1916

Sarah Cohen, courtesy Lewis Herlitz

14 THE SOUTHEND AND WESTCLIFF GRAPHIC. December 19, 1913.

George Wilkins

:: Departmental Stores. ::

Special Christmas Lines.

GROCERY

Muscatels .. .. per lb. 1/- & 1/4
Jordan Almonds .. ,, 1/11 & 2/6
Figs .. .. .. ,, 4½d. & 6d.
,, in Boxes 6½d., 7½d., 11½d. & 1/8
,, Pulled, in Boxes 11½d. 1/3 & 1/9
Chyloong's Ginger per jar 7½d., 1/4½, & 2/4½d.
Finest Icing Sugar .. .. per lb. 3½d.
Flavouring Essences .. per 1 oz. bot. 5½d.
Pastry Whites .. 7 lb. bag 11½d.
Victoria Plums .. per bot. 7½d.
Yellow Plums .. ,, 6½d.

PROVISION

English Cheese a speciality.
All from First Prize Dairies.
Stilton, Fine Ripe (whole cheese) per lb. 1/3
Cheddar .. .. .. ,, 11d.
Cheddar Loaves .. .. ,, 11d.
Cheshire, White or Coloured ,, 11d.
Derby .. .. ,, 11d.
Caerphilly .. .. .. ,, 9d.
Double Gloucester .. .. ,, 11d.
Single Gloucester .. .. ,, 11d.
North Wilts .. .. ,, 11d.
Wensleydale .. .. .. ,, 1/3

The Stiltons were made by Mrs. Skinner, of Melton Mowbray, who took the Champion prize in the Lord Mayor's Cup for the best cheese in the London Dairy Show.

CONFECTIONERY

Bonbons all prices, from 4½d. to 2/6.
A large assortment of Cadbury's and other makers Chocolates in Fancy and full-weight boxes at special prices. See Windows.
Keillers Assorted Chocolates per 2 lb. box 1/10½
,, Texas Mixture per 2 lb. box 1/3
Clarnico Victoria Mixture per lb. box 6½d.

GREEN FRUIT

A choice selection of Hot House Grapes and Californian Newtown Pippins at Lowest Prices.

Domestic Ironmongery

An excellent assortment of domestic ironmongery, brooms and brushes, always in stock.

George Wilkins
Grocer & Provision Merchant
Hamlet Court Rd. WESTCLIFF-ON-SEA

From *Southend and Westcliff Graphic* 1913

ROBERT PAYN,

MILLINER, COSTUMIER AND FANCY DRAPER,

Noted House for **Blouses, Jackets, Mantles, Costumes, Costume Skirts** (extra large and small sizes a speciality) of which the largest, best and most fashionable stock in the neighbourhood is held.

TOWER BUILDINGS, 75, HIGH ST., & 1, CLIFF TOWN RD.

For Mantles, Costumes and Blouses.

Mourning Orders

executed with greatest promptitude.

LONDON HOUSE 13 CLIFF TOWN R

For Millinery, Hosiery, Laces, Umbrellas, Furs, Haberdashery, &

Orders by Post, Telephone or Telegram pro executed.

LATEST FASHIONS,
LARGEST ASSORTMEN
LOWEST PRICES.

Telephone No. 16Y5 SOUTHEND.

SOUTHEND-ON-SE

From *Mates Illustrated Guide to Southend-on-Sea* 1907

Southend bathers between wars, **courtesy Gail Durbin**

Above: Governess lurking behind Edwardian family, Chalkwell Park
courtesy Lynn Tait

Right: From *Southend and Westcliff Graphic* 1895

Above: Family's Hospital, Shoebury

Left: Advertisement promoting health benefits, 1936, **courtesy Southend Standard**

Corporation Hot & Cold Sea Water Baths

ALSO FRESH WATER BATHS MEDICAL, OZONE & IODIZED

PIER HILL BUILDINGS

Adjoining Pier Entrance.

Telephone 49452.

Comfortable Rest Rooms. Facing South.

Open 1st April to 30th September—
Weekdays and Sundays 7 a.m. to 7.15 p.m.

October, November & March—
Weekdays 8 a.m. to 7.15 p.m.
Sundays 8 a.m. to 12.30 p.m.

December, January, February—
Sundays to Fridays (inclusive) 8 a.m. to 2 p.m.
Saturdays - - - 8 a.m. to 6 p.m.

These celebrated Medical Baths have been found to be especially efficacious for Rheumatism, Gout, Liver Derangements, Indigestion, etc. They improve the action of the Skin, Invigorate the circulation and give tone to the General Health.

Ultra Violet Ray available for special treatment.

The Baths are patronised by the leading Football Clubs when training for Cup-tie Matches, etc.

OZONE IODIZED BATHS 5/-

Books of Twelve Tickets £2/10/0.

(To avoid waiting, one hour's notice should be given so that Bath can be prepared).

SEA WATER OR FRESH WATER BATHS (Hot or Cold).

First-Class Private Baths 1/6 each with 2 Towels and Soap. Second-Class Private Baths 9d. each with 1 Towel and Soap. Use of Extra Towels 1d. each.

Books containing Twelve 1/6 Tickets, 15/-.

Books containing Twelve 9d. Tickets, 7/6.

The Corporation will not be responsible for any articles left in the Dressing Rooms.

Children under 12 Half Price.

Special arrangements for Football and Athletic Clubs, School and other Parties.

Private Baths reserved and prepared for any hour upon Telephone Message to Piermaster's Office.

SOUTHEND, 6188

SOUTHEND-ON-SEA.

Young Ladies' Physical and Gymnastic Class.

A SELECT LADIES' GYMNASTIC CLASS will take place on FRIDAY EVENINGS from 6.30 to 8 p.m. at the Westcliff Institute, corner of Argyll Road, Westcliff-on-Sea, trams pass door of Institute from Southend and Leigh. The Ladies will be taught Club-swinging, Dumb-bell, Bar-bell, Vaulting Horse and Parallel Bar Exercises, Fancy and Figure Marching, Running Drills and Free Gymnastic Exercises with music. Ladies not required to bring Clubs. etc. Hon. Sec., Miss D.E. HOOFF, Holmwood College, Hamlet Court Road. Instructor, Colour-Sergt. W. PECK, 35, Ambleside Drive, Southend-on-Sea. Pattern of Ladies' Gymnastic Uniform from Hon. Sec. or Instructor.

A GENTLEMEN'S FENCING (FOILS) CLASS at 8.15 p.m., after Ladies' Class.

FENCING.

Colour-Sergt. W. PECK, 35, Ambleside Drive, gives private lessons in Foil Fencing to Ladies and Gentlemen. Also Physical and Gymnastic Classes for young Ladies, Boys and Girls. Prospectus on application.

Above: From *Southend and Westcliff Graphic* 1908

Right: Mutoscope

Absalom's bathing machine

From *Southend and Westcliff Graphic* 1913

Leigh Regatta 1925

Women on Southend Pier, 1930s, **courtesy Nick Skinner**

Suffragettes in Southend, **courtesy Docklands Museum**

Suffrage postcard

Augusta Tawke, courtesy Peter Brown

Suffragette postcard 1913

The effect of first lady councillor from *Southend and Westcliff Graphic* 1910

Local baby clinic, First World War

hoeing turnips. Allotments became particularly popular during and after the First World War, with working girls giving up their spare time to cultivate land or help out at local farms.

Seafood, of course, was readily available, cash permitting, from local fishermen – including oysters; by 1875, Leigh-on-Sea was also famous for its cockles. With access to some kind of shotgun, there was also the option of catching and eating birds – including sparrows. Generally, as elsewhere, bread was the staple diet of the nineteenth century, topped up (again, cash permitting) with small amounts of vegetables and cheese from local farms, plus lard and, of course, tea. A luxury such as butter was available from such sources as Mrs Braye, a local dairywoman, selling her wares for no less than 2*s* per lb in the 1870s. Sausages were the speciality of Shelley's in Rochford, advertising in the *Southend Standard and Essex Weekly Advertiser,* 3 October 1889, and described as from 'young pigs, fatted at the Dairy Farm of Mr C. Tabor', praised as late as 1913 in a privately published book, *Hunting Recollections.* Shelley's also advertised their homemade brawn, 'home-picked' (*sic* – pickled?) ox tongues, and prime pickled pork as well as bargain priced butter at just 1*s* per lb and oranges at fifty for 1*s*. For those who preferred rabbit, there was a specialist in Queen's Road, Southend, at the Farmers' Direct Supply Company, advertising in the same newspaper in 1898. As for fresh water, there were water carriers hawking their wares around the streets of Southend until the last half of the nineteenth century, with just a few pumps available – as in Leigh-on-Sea and Prittlewell – although some farms had their own wells. Such was the precious nature of water, that at least one of the local pumps was locked for certain hours per day to conserve its precious contents. A Health Committee meeting of April 1894 refused Miss Scratton's request for a hydrant for the tenants at the cottages she owned in Prittlewell because they could see that what was needed was a proper independent supply leading to each cottage.

Alcohol was often easier to get hold of than safe drinking water, causing its own particular problems – with Southend sporting its own brewery in Luker Road from 1869. A local branch of the British Women's Temperance Association was initiated in the town with 220 members by 1895, culminating in a well-attended lecture in Victoria Hall in Alexandra Street in October 1900. Alderman Burrows referred to the number of establishments selling liquor in the town, and suggested that this was because of the demand 'by women for liquor for home drinking', and because in public houses, even if the landlord recommended tea (!), local women were favouring gin two or three times over. The lecturer, Mrs Osborn, President of the National Association, 'deplored the frequenting of public houses by women' and remarked upon its 'frequency' at Southend and spoke of cases of girl drunkenness which had come under her observation in the High Street. This is backed up by the number of drunk and disorderly cases reported in the local press – there were two cases in one day at Rochford Petty Session in June 1883, both women charged with being drunk on the highway. Charlotte Whittingham was fined 5*s* plus 7*s* costs, and Susannah Crane fined 10*s* and costs or 14 days in prison if in default. In January 1888, Emma Kirby was fined 10*s* and 13*s* 6*d* costs for the same offence, with further fines of £1 plus 13*s* 6*d* when she repeated the offence in October, with Rosina Searle fined 9*s* and locked up for the night in March 1907 after being found 'drunk in Southchurch Avenue' and pleading guilty to 'having a little drink'. The nearest prison, incidentally, was in Chelmsford, a long journey by horse-drawn carriage, although archivists at Essex Record Office surmise that prisoners – accompanied – may well have been required to walk the twenty miles.

In 1900, the local Women's Temperance group had obtained the signatures of 2,164 Southend women asking the Licensing Justices not to grant a licence for the pier. In 1905, another 1,630 signatures were obtained objecting to any further licences for grocers in Southend to sell 'strong drink.' They felt that 'the respectable trade of the grocer serves as a cover to the dangerous one of the liquor seller'. Again, this is supported by such stories in the local press as that of Mary Ann Garnham of Shoeburyness, charged with 'unlawfully selling intoxicating liquors ... without being duly licensed' in July 1891 and being fined £2 plus 10*s* 6*d* costs. In February 1909, the saloon-smashing American, Carrie Nation, visited Southend and gave a talk to 'women only' at the Summercourt Hall in Westcliff, followed by a mixed audience later the same day. She had taken a hatchet to smash 'the doors of hell' – a public house – and was unapologetic for her action against these 'hell-holes' which ruined men's lives and broke mothers' hearts. Mrs Nation claimed to be in favour of abolishing drink altogether rather than claiming to be a temperance advocate, and was convinced that the solving of the drink question would solve the unemployed question. However, the closest Britain came to prohibition was during the First World War, when pub hours became subject to licences, the alcohol content was reduced and tax on alcoholic drinks was raised. By 1914, the National Temperance Association was promoting the king's example of banishing all intoxicating liquor from the home for the period of the war. In the *Southend and Westcliff Graphic* of 30 April 1915, there was an appeal to members of the Leigh-on-Sea Lodge of Good Templars to pledge themselves to do all in their power to discourage the use of alcohol as a beverage. This may not have been that successful, given that in 1927, the National British Women's Total Abstinence Union estimated that Southend's drink bill was £843,310 for that year (£6 15*s* 3*d* per head, equivalent to £413 per head in 2018) – they subsequently opened a milk bar in the High Street in 1936, but, again, how effective this was is difficult to define. The Band of Hope – discouraging children from consuming alcohol – was also active in the area during and after the First World War, with a worthy aim but unknown results.

In the town in the nineteenth century, women were not just being charged with alcohol-induced offences. Other offences reveal some of the desperation induced by poverty – as when Mary Ann Pittingale of Eastwood (near Southend) was charged with stealing two 'peeks' of potatoes growing in a field, the property of James Tabor who was a member of the Bench hearing the case in November 1862. He promptly retired from the proceedings, but the case was proven and Mary was fined 10*s* being the 1*s* value of the potatoes and 8*s* – plus costs – which she paid rather than face fourteen days in prison. In March 1888, hungry Emily Wells from Runwell Terrace stole a tin of salmon value 9*d*, and was fined 20*s* or fourteen days' imprisonment. Then there was Catherine Miltson, an inmate of Rochford workhouse in 1882, who refused to work and was sent to prison for fourteen days, and homeless Eliza Hills who was charged with sleeping in an outhouse on 6 October 1888 in Southend, and sentenced to two months' imprisonment with hard labour; harsh times indeed. Isabella Tusson was fined £1 for stealing and pawning linen from the Royal Sanitary Laundry where she was engaged in 1896, a more lenient sentence as times moved on. Enterprising (and presumably homeless) 17-year-old Maria Gione was charged in 1897 with obtaining goods from various tradesmen by pretending she had been sent by the Mother Superior of Nazareth House, a local children's home, and was remanded until the Catholic curate managed to find a home for her. However, it was a woman who pointed out to the Highways and Works Committee in August 1896 that the residents of York Road and Southchurch Avenue in particular needed a police presence and 'more police protection in the neighbourhood' – with women more likely to be the victim than the offender. While this is no doubt true, there were still plenty of women in trouble for petty theft well into the twentieth century. In May, 1917, for example, three local girls (Lilian Hurst, 20, of Seaview Road, Dorothy Brooks, 21, of Queens Road, and Emily Himpett, 21, a domestic servant also from Queens Road) stole £2 10*s* and a cashbox from a Queens Road carpenter and a purse plus 6*s* 8*d* from Brightwell Avenue and were all sent to prison. Brooks and Himpett had a clean record and served fourteen days, but Hurst, who had been on probation for stealing boots six years earlier and had since been deserted by her Canadian husband who paid no support, received twenty-eight days' hard labour.

As the town's population expanded, shops began to open – notably, those in Nelson Street from 1860, adjacent to the

Clifftown Estate which was being developed close to Southend Central Station complete with a water supply, replacing cornfields which still extended beyond Royal Terrace. This was also the time when food imports increased although it was still unlikely that poor families could afford meat more than once a week – but in fact the working class Victorian free-from-preservatives diet was relatively healthy and both men and women were more physically active out of necessity. Domestic staff working long hours, women doing their own laundry, the necessity of walking (or, latterly, perhaps cycling) everywhere, women helping out on local farms to earn a few pence – little opportunity to sit with their feet up, especially with a clutch of children at home to care for. In fact, some poor families became even poorer following the Agricultural Gangs Act of 1867 which made it illegal to employ children under 8 years of age, thereby depriving them of a potential breadwinner – although this was good news for the children.

Canon King's wife – in the 1880s – was in the fortunate position of not only having servants, but of being able to grow her own flowers and vegetables, mentioning poppies, sweet peas, roses, cucumbers, peas, parsnips and cherries. In her letters she also refers to the grapes and peaches flourishing in her greenhouses.

An interesting entry in the *Southend Standard* of 28 December 1899 refers to the cookery classes at the local Technical Institute, complaining that the stipulation for students to use 'the highest quality ingredients' and 'nicely regulated gas stoves' is too costly for working class cookery.

> With regard to the treacle cake and rhubarb pudding, Irish stew, frying fish … on the syllabus, I submit that the inclusion of any one of these in the category of working class cookery must inevitably depend upon the requisite utensils and cost incurred … I admit they are generally toothsome, but neither economical, satisfying, nor conducive to the health of a bilious temperament.

There are a number of recipes printed in nineteenth-century copies of the *Southend Standard and Essex Weekly Advertiser*. A January, 1884, issue has such delicacies as 'Venison Steaks on Toast', and 'Sweetbreads', plus 'White Muffins'. In May 1898, there are six ways to cook macaroni, including a fried (!) version. In 1906, working-class women could buy a locally produced cookery book (published by the New Congregational Church in Westcliff-on-Sea) which featured 125 recipes, including 'Nice Supper Dish' (an onion, sheep's kidney and butter), 'Rabbit Cream' (a rabbit, breadcrumbs, milk, butter and one egg), 'Five Minutes Pudding' (flour, sugar, eggs and baking powder), and – perhaps rather surprisingly – 'Onion and Celery Porridge'!

In 1904, a Government Commission report on the typical working-class diet showed that bread and butter was the favoured breakfast, potatoes and herrings the most popular 'dinner' with bread and butter for 'tea'. A little more money meant small quantities of pork, mutton and beef, all now available from the established butchers in Nelson Street and in the expanding High Street, which was now slowly being dominated by Mr Garon and his growing chain of shops selling pretty much everything.

During the early part of the First World War, a Mrs Crick of 14 Royal Terrace (an expensive part of Southend) was buying household groceries from local shops on credit, the shops issuing her with a book listing all her purchases, which she settled monthly. She was spending £1 per month on bread and biscuits from H. Ackerman in Nelson Street, and averaging over £4 per month on meat from Joseph Webster, Purveyor of Meat in Clifftown Road. By 1918, there was a market in York Road offering low prices for different household budgets, welcomed by local women who had lost their husbands, or who were unemployed or in ill health. Cheaper still was homemade blackbird pie or eels caught locally, popular during this period.

It is not just housing and food that give an insight into how women in Southend were living (and for some, struggling) between 1850 and 1950. A look at how they were dressing is also relevant. Whether any local women became part of the Rational Dress Movement in the mid-1800s is not clear. The movement opposed tight corsets and impractical and unwieldy skirts, as damaging to health and inhumane – with such constrictions reflecting women's restricted lives. The growth in the use of bicycles locally would have made such changes in women's clothing very welcome.

Alexandra Street – off the High Street – was also developing as a shopping area, with a branch of Bon Marché advertising in *Where To Buy at Southend* in 1891. This was a specifically constructed four-storey building for the business which had grown out of its Nelson Street premises – with windows dressed 'in peculiarly good taste', showing 'attractive and stylish' goods aimed at the female shopper. There were 'dress, mantle and millinery departments … conducted quite in accordance with the spirit of the times'.

While there are few specific references to what women were wearing locally if they did not have the resources to shop at such retailers as Bon Marché, they would have had options at local jumble sales or even the local visiting rag-man. Repairing and darning clothes was something even non-seamstresses could handle, and dark colours were favoured at the bottom of the social scale because they didn't show the dirt. Women who wore caps and bonnets were not necessarily adhering to fashion or the notion of respectability, but to keep hair from getting caught in machines or to fend off head-lice. Middle- and upper-class women would keep abreast of fashion with articles in the *Southend Standard and Essex Weekly Advertiser* – one issue dated 6 March 1890 enthuses about braided military jackets and fur tippets, wraps made of brocade and velvet with feather trims and satin linings. Hats were pretty much an essential accessory until well into the twentieth century, and this same article itemises shapes such as the Toreador and the Paul Jones, pointing out the popularity of trimmings (which made the hats more versatile). Such trimmings are also mentioned in a self-published booklet by David Jones on the subject of Milton Road in Westcliff-on-Sea in 1905, when lady assistants in a drapers called Knight's would take time discussing which artificial flowers were best suited to the hat being purchased.

Another writer recollecting Southend in 1865 (Augusta Tawke) showed quite an interest in the appearance of the 'excursionists' who were described as 'large and fat with scarlet faces, their skirt and bodice parting company', wearing 'enormous hats with drooping white plumes'. Residents 'of rank and fashion', however, were recalled as meeting at the library (then opposite the Royal Hotel, offering more than just books), with elderly ladies dressed in 'black satin or velvet'. Miss Tawke also refers to women 'arrayed in all the glory of silk skirts with gathers, lace shawls, bonnets with ribbon strings tied under the chin, and enormous crinolines', watching outdoor activities. Favoured footwear was the button boot, and boots could be repaired or exchanged at Dolphin's Boot and Umbrella Hospital in Market Place.

As the years passed, more women were wearing a uniform at work, including attendants in the public toilets, and, after the First World War, in the newly built library in Victoria Avenue (initially black stockings and black overalls). The unfortunate women in the local workhouse, of course, had no choice but to wear a shapeless, hard-wearing uniform of a coarse calico shift, with a 'P' for pauper. Families who still employed servants in 1906 could purchase 'maids' dresses, caps and aprons' from Robert W. Goodchild, a draper in Hamlet Court Road. Interestingly, the shop still sold corsets – perhaps aware of those who were anti the Rational Dress Movement, claiming that corsets promoted good posture and social status. Those who had joined the Women's Land Army disagreed with this idea, in that the steel bones in corsets were prone to rust in part due to the rain and in part to the inevitable unladylike perspiration they experienced!

During the First World War, and in spite of what was happening locally in terms of Zeppelin activity, bombs being dropped and anti-aircraft guns etc., the *Southend and Westcliff Graphic* continued to appeal to their female readers via their advertisements. Corsets, manicures, chiropody, facial massage, hairdressers, and skin creams with such by-lines as Vinolia's 'Beauty on Duty has a Duty to Beauty', all featured regularly. Lipstick was never mentioned, and it seems that it was considered 'fast' and 'French' – until munitionettes started wearing it to cheer up their dreary uniforms. By the end of the 1920s, there were indications of the changes in women's underwear – while Percy Raven's traditional store in Hamlet Court Road (Westcliff) was advertising 'The Boston Garter' as the correct garment for all occasions, with 'unrustable fittings', the parish magazine of St Mary's (Prittlewell) was advertising 'Lovely Lingerie' from Inverness Avenue, 'hand embroidered by Irish peasants'(!). Although 'Make Do And Mend' became a slogan for women during the Second World War, the concept had been around for many years before. If you were a wartime bride, you would probably have to collect clothing coupons from friends and family to have enough for a wedding dress, unless you picked up one of those donated by incoming Americans for war brides. Hats – an essential part of any outfit in those days – were, interestingly, not rationed, but turn-ups were abolished from trousers because of the 'waste'.

For winter, furriers were very much in evidence between the wars, with Hampton's in Hamlet Court Road selling 'the largest selection of furs in England'. For summer, bathing costumes were becoming briefer, and from 1932, a swimwear parade was held on the pier. From as early as 1949 however, some local women were objecting to using flashes of flesh to boost product sales; twins Irene and Rita Day from Merilies Gardens, Westcliff, refused to be filmed in bathing suits when they were hired to advertise hair products.

Although women made progress in relation to their mode of dress, and slowly acquired rights with regard to their property, salaries and their 'voice', divorce settlements were slow to catch up, being the prerogative of the rich in the Victorian era. Women had made some progress since 1855 at which time they lost everything they owned on their wedding day and were unable to sign contracts or make a will. In 1857, the Matrimonial Causes Act meant that 'ordinary' people could divorce without it costing a fortune, including, for example, Mrs Mary Newell, the wife of the proprietor of the Bon Marche drapers, who was granted a decree nisi in 1899 on the grounds of his cruelty. Not that this solved all marital problems, but divorce certainly proliferated after another Matrimonial Causes Act in 1923. This established equality between the sexes in divorce cases, and made divorce more accessible to poorer people. By 1937, a matrimonial court in Southend had been set up and was meeting weekly.

Before the twentieth century however, marriage was still seen as the best way for a woman to secure an income, but there was a lot of competition for this role. When local historian Philip Benton lost his wife in 1874, he had a few possible replacements in mind and let his nine children choose which one should take over their late mother's role. They chose the governess, Miss Warren, which seemed to work out to be a satisfactory arrangement for all concerned.

Certainly, marriage remained more popular than cohabiting during the century covered by this book, and, compared to divorces, details of local marriages took up plenty of space in local newspapers. These accounts, yet again, are often class-led – the more guests, the more prominent the groom, the more extravagant the wedding, the more likely it was to be reported. Take the wedding of Miss Thackeray in 1879, for example, the daughter of the Rev. Frederick Thackeray (cousin of William Makepeace Thackeray) of 9 Royal Terrace; she was attended by nine bridesmaids, with eight carriages required to convey guests to the church at Prittlewell. The *Chelmsford Chronicle* of 8 June reported that the bride wore white satin with a tulle veil and the bridesmaids wore white satin and lace. Sixty guests attended a reception at the Royal Hotel, with a special train apparently organised for some of these guests, the bride and her new husband (Dr Francis Bernard) returning on this train to London and thence to Belgium for their honeymoon. It also describes the town and the station as being ornamented with bunting as part of the celebrations! As well as describing the new Mrs Bernard's travelling outfit (ruby cashmere trimmed with ruby and grey stamped velvet with hand-painted buttons), there was half a column devoted to a list of the wedding gifts – everything from a claret jug to a chess set, from an inkstand to a Chinese antimacassar to a silver sardine box.

The well-known attitude towards marriage depicted in Jane Austen's popular novels had not entirely dissipated. Daniel Scratton, local squire and landowner who lived in Royal Terrace before the end of the nineteenth century would make such observations as 'There they go, off to market again', should a family with two marriageable daughters pass him by, although suffragettes would not have been regarded as marriage material of course. However, not so many years later, one spirited chambermaid who had been working at the Westcliff Hotel, Charlotte Saunders, took her ex-fiance, William Blaney, to court for breach of promise. She had had her wedding plans foiled in 1908 when her 'beau' had broken off their engagement with the words: 'I don't want you, and I don't care for you.' This feisty young woman won her case, securing £35 damages (*Southend Standard and Essex Weekly Advertiser* of 26 November 1908.) Incidentally, local women in the 1930s had the option of getting married in a very unusual venue – the mouth of Eric, the embalmed whale on display at the Kursaal!

While women were marrying (and in some cases divorcing) between the wars, they were also beginning to benefit from Acts of Parliament – old age pensions were payable from 1925 (for the over 65s) as was widows' benefit, and eighteenth-century child tax allowances had been re-introduced before the First World War. The image of the 1920s as being a time of 'flappers' and fun did not apply to all of Southend's women. In June 1927, five women were summoned for touting for lodgers at Southend Central station and 'bound over' for six months, while a year later Georgina Brown of Clifftown Road was charged with keeping a house of ill repute. There had been a complaint about the latter from Mrs Lodge of the Railway Restaurant because what went on was 'too disgraceful for anyone to live next to', and the occupants of the basement flat had also complained of 'noisy conduct'. On the night before the police raided the premises, thirty men were said to have entered the house. Mrs Brown was sent to prison for two months hard labour, and the three girls found on the premises were also sent to prison for between six weeks and two months hard labour – all of them responded with shrieks as they left the court according to the *Essex Newsman* (4 August).

However, there were advances for some women, nationally and locally, between the wars. Women were driving cars, and even learning to fly, with varying degrees of success. The *Chelmsford Chronicle* of 20 March 1936 gave an account of a 'Westcliff Lady Driver Summoned' for driving a motor car dangerously at East Horndon. Mrs Helen Pryor of Drake Road had crashed into a stationary vehicle because she 'did not see the stop light', and her footbrake did not work – which was subsequently confirmed to be the case when a bolt or pin was found to be missing. The Bench considered it 'a bad and serious case of dangerous driving', and Mrs Pryor was fined £10 with £4 6*s* 10*d* costs, and disqualified from driving for six months. Amy Johnson, no less, was taught to fly by Captain Froude R. Matthews from Thorpe Bay in 1928, qualifying in 1929. She of course crashed in 1941 into the Thames estuary at nearby Foulness.

It took a while for women to get used to the danger of the motor car with reports in the *Southend Standard* in the 1920s of women chatting in the middle of the road in the path of a council steam roller (which managed to avoid them – and their prams) and of a woman crossing the road with an umbrella obscuring her view, this time not avoiding the vehicle which hit and killed her. The trams which had been established in 1901 were replaced by buses in 1932, and these were generally more popular with the womenfolk until after the Second World War.

In *The Girls of Southend High School 1913–2013*, Pam Mansell wrote of the different approaches of speakers at the school through the 1920s and 30s, with Judge Sherwell Cooper in 1929 pointing out that girls had the world at their feet, while the Bishop of Chelmsford in 1930 spoke of a decline in decorum, in line with the Free Church Council's description of Southend in the '20s as a 'centre of revelry, licence, disregard of decencies … a hotbed of Saturnalia'. This latter description was a reference to the briefer clothing now worn in and around the beaches, and to yet more instances of drunk and disorderly women being prosecuted. Local newspapers are the source of such instances

– *The Newsman* of 2 April 1921, for instance, reported that Norah Seager, a barmaid, had been found in Beedell Avenue by P.C. Bryant, so drunk that she had to be 'supported by a sailor'; she was fined 10*s*.

The depression during the 1930s affected women in Southend as much as anywhere, but the town council was certainly trying to make life more comfortable for residents, as well as looking after the increasing number of visitors. Help for the poorer women of the town regularly came from another local provider: the Southend Civic Guild of Help in Clarence Road, a forerunner of the Citizens' Advice Bureau, established in 1908, and offering practical help as well as advice. At their annual meeting detailed in the *Essex County Chronicle* which was held at the Palace Hotel in October 1912, the Chairman referred to the work being done by 'a large number of ladies … to give very largely of their time, advice and help to the poorer part of the population', with '311 new cases considered and 103 cases of necessitous children investigated for the Education Care Committee.' The Guild's annual reports at Southend's Forum (library) are very revealing – a few cases follow:

1936 – Found suitable accommodation for young woman recovering from tuberculosis, who was able to work after a few months, with her earnings topped up by the Guild's TB Care Committee to enable her to buy milk and Ovaltine.

1937 – A 55-year-old woman who was supplementing her small income with needlework but who needed spectacles had them funded by the Guild, repaying them in part by instalments.

1938 – A 17-year-old girl with infantile paralysis in urgent need of a new surgical boot and shoe, costing £3 10*s*, had this paid for by the Guild with the assistance of the Royal Surgical Aid Society, because her father had left the family home and was not contributing financially.

1939 – cases included helping two women to pay for dentures: a widow and 'an invalid woman'. (Requests for clothing that year had substantially exceeded supply, although

> over 4,500 garments and 644 pairs of boots had been distributed.)

Thus, although better housing, a new hospital and more leisure facilities were all projects completed between the wars, not everyone had access to such improvements.

However, in times of depression, or uncertainty, it is not unusual, for women in particular, to turn to fortune-telling for reassurance, and this was the case in Southend. In 1906, 'Madame Nora' was fined 40*s* plus 4*s* costs for practising palmistry at the Kursaal. Seances also became particularly popular during the wars, and such local bazaars as those organised by St Saviour's Church in Westcliff featured palmists as one of the attractions – in 1938 for instance, it was 'The Lady From Egypt.' This was one area where money could be earned fraudulently, telling women what they wanted to hear. In 1916, the *Chelmsford Chronicle* of 2 June refers to five local women 'pretending to tell fortunes with intent to deceive'. These were named only by their 'professional' names as Madame Churchill, Madame Marguerite, Madame Roberts, Madame Keiro and Madame Leena. Arrests and fines were no deterrent in the years that followed. There were another five prosecutions reported in the issue of 24 January 1936, featuring 'Madame Rosa' – revealed as the widow of local illusionist The Great Rameses – 'Madame Zena', otherwise Alice Fisher of London Road, Westcliff, who told the court she was 'regularly employed at the mayor's garden parties', 'Madame Corona', otherwise Annie Corona of Church Road, Southend, 'Madame Astral', otherwise Marion Arding of Queen's Road, Southend, and 'Madame St Aubyn', otherwise Lynn Perhan of Belleview (*sic*) Road, Southend. Evidence for these prosecutions was given by police clerk Catherine Turner, and 'assistant police matron' Harriet Cannon, revealing that Madame Rosa produced a crystal claimed to have come from King Tutankhamen's tomb, all the women predicting long lives for those 'crossing their palm with silver'. They were all fined £2 with 10*s* costs.

Local women were also appearing in court during the First World War for more innocent offences. Even Essex girls married to 'aliens' had to register, along with their husbands, but Kate Iberti, married to an Italian, was unaware of this. She was living at the Royal Hotel in February 1915 (as per the *Southend on Sea Observer*) and her status meant that she was interviewed by a detective inspector. She had failed to register, but complained that the hotel should have informed her of this, because she now felt 'such a German' – as a result, the case was dismissed and she registered as required. Similarly, in April 1915 (according to the *Southend and Westcliff Graphic* 30 April), Elizabeth Knight, boarding-house keeper of Trinity Avenue, was summoned for failing to notify the Alien Registration Officer of aliens in her household. Her case too was withdrawn, as it was felt that her appearance in court would be sufficient to serve as a deterrent to others. However, it does not seem to have worked, as three other landladies were fined for failing to give notice of the presence of aliens in their accommodation the following month. There were also a number of cases in 1915 of landladies fined for failing to obscure indoor lighting, with forty-eight cases recorded in July and 130 in August that year, all fined around £12. A lower fine of £2 was even imposed on Mrs Annie Swan, the Matron of the Glen Hospital in Southchurch Road, for the same reason in December – lower because it was Christmas or because it was a hospital is not known.

In 1940, 84,000 Southend residents left the town, although many returned within a year – apart from the men and women who joined the Armed Forces of course. Pregnant women were excluded from returning, partly due to a shortage of doctors in the town. The question of women's rights was overtaken by an emphasis on survival, as in the First World War, especially as Southend was so vulnerable on the cusp of the estuary, where German bombers jettisoned any bombs left over after bombing London. There was one female corporal, Gerry Kelly of the Experimental Assistants in Gunnery at Shoeburyness, who did her bit for women, though, war or no war. She was put on a charge for wearing gunners' battledress instead of the standard navy blue skirt and pullover – but Colonel Lickman rather liked the idea, so that all EAGs were instructed to follow Gerry's example.

As for wartime weddings, women such as Doris Patience relied on family donations of clothing coupons – although her father was a grocer and able to accumulate much of the food and drink she needed for her reception at home in Southend in 1943, with left-over booze put to good use on VE Day. Another bride who married at St Helen's Church in Milton Road in 1941 had a Spam wedding breakfast at the Palace Hotel. Because of the rationing in force, wedding cake was not readily available, but the happy couple declined an offer of a cardboard replica! It seems that lace was not rationed, however, and the wedding dress was homemade from blue lace hunted out in a London store.

Women who needed support after the war could turn to one of several local organisations stepping in to help those seriously disadvantaged by the years of hardship, losing their family and/or their home, or were just struggling financially. The Royal Artillery Association (set up in Southend in 1944) was one such organisation. In 1945, for instance, they obtained a grant for furniture for the wife of a gunner who had been a prisoner of war in Japan; they also bought a pram for another gunner's wife, and a doll for another's daughter. The Southend Civic Guild for Help was back in action from 1948 – one example during that year was of a woman whose husband's job and salary at a local factory had been downgraded from £9 to £4-£6 per week, with hire purchase debts of £4 per week, two young children to fund, and another baby on the way. The Guild made her a loan so she could buy a layette and second-hand pram for the new baby. Another example was the funding of a new oven in 1949 for a woman living in a small cottage 'in the middle of the fields' at Rochford – a woman who had not had a hot meal for many months. A year later, they stepped in when a grandmother who had lost her son during the war was concerned about the mistreatment of her 4-year-old grandson by his stepfather. She had taken him in and the cost of caring for him was stretching her financially; the Guild called on the assistance of the RAF Benevolent Fund to help in this case. So, while the Family Allowance Act of 1945, the National Insurance Act of 1946 and the National Health Act of 1948 (among others) improved finances for some, other women were still struggling, and still living in houses without indoor toilets, baths or hot water. A lot left to fight for.

CHAPTER FOUR

Health

In the mid-nineteenth century, Southend-on-Sea was regarded as a particularly healthy place to live, aspiring to be a spa town as publicised by visits from Queen Caroline and Princess Louise some years before. Nazareth House in London's Hammersmith sent their most infirm, or incurable, children to benefit from the sea air at the home which they had opened in Westcliff Parade in 1873 as a place of rest and convalescence for not only sick children but other sick members of the congregation, including the elderly. Demand soon outgrew the building, necessitating a move to an old manor house, Milton Hall, in London Road after a couple of years. Local people contributed bread, meat, groceries, straw for bedding, and material for clothing – and a cow. According to a 1930 pamphlet on the subject at Essex Records Office in Chelmsford, by 1901 the home had taken in some lady residents 'of a better class' who had their own 'fine sitting room'; the pamphlet also has an image of an elderly woman, bonneted and cloaked, seated in state upon a red velvet ottoman and described as 'happily crazed … waiting for the King to call for her in a hurry to walk abroad'.

The nuns of Nazareth House – which dates back to 1873 – also took in abandoned babies who were left in a metal cradle, known as the foundling cradle, built into their boundary wall. Placing the baby in the cradle activated a bell to ensure the baby received attention from the nuns, but without divulging the identity of the parent(s). Mothers who were so poor they could not feed, or simply did not want, their (often illegitimate) babies, could place them in the rigid cradle, turn it round to face away from the road, and pull down a metal grille to protect their anonymity. This was not the only place that babies arrived unexpectedly, as any doorstep would do in an emergency. One case in the *Chelmsford Chronicle* of 16 March 1894 features Alice Clements who abandoned her baby on a doorstep in Wilson Road on 21 December, having given birth in London. Alice, 34, had been living in Southend, and appears to have changed her mind shortly after the abandonment, but when she retraced her steps, the baby had been taken to the police station and from there to the workhouse. She was charged and tried, resulting in a fine of £5 with £1 0*s* 6*d* costs or fourteen days in prison if she defaulted.

Southend was regarded as a healthy destination for East Enders in particular. John Kirk from the Ragged School Union wrote to the *Southend Standard and Essex Weekly Advertiser* in July 1908 expressing his gratitude for local fundraising events by the 'unflagging friends of the Home and the children'. The RSU had maintained a presence in the town by this time for fifteen years, with a home then on Southchurch Beach erected specifically, the foundation stone laid by Princess Louise in 1895. About 300 children a year enjoyed an annual holiday at The Cripples' Home, as it was known, which also took on long term residents. A similar organisation, the Sunshine Home for the Poor at Shoeburyness, which took on 'crippled and badly nourished children from the poorest part of the East End' was also established in 1929, but, as children's health improved, became a hostel in 1948, and a care home later.

In the *London Evening Standard* of October 1907, the Vicar of Plaistow appealed for funds to send the 'sick and invalid poor generally of this large East End parish of 27,000 who need fresh air, medical advice and good nursing during convalescence' to St Monica's or St Mary's Holiday Homes in Southend. Three years later, he crops up again in the *East London Observer* referring to a 'human stream of Plaistow children and women making its way to the holiday homes … at Southend'. He wrote of his hope that:

> there would have been no need to … appeal for assistance for the upkeep of these health factories but the absence of summer has had a disastrous effect upon funds that must be maintained by friends, who sometimes forget

> that, though the weather be unpropitious, even a change of rain is of inestimable value to those who must dwell in London.

St Monica's also operated a refuge for girls in need of care and protection from 1899 at various addresses over the years. In 1904 this became known as Southend Girls' Refuge after the Rev. Varney at St John's in the town centre was shocked by the number of girls sleeping in the streets nearby. Subsequently, girls were sent to the home by the local Women's Patrol and the police. In November 1929, the Chelmsford Diocesan Association for Girls' Aid met in Leigh to discuss the rescue work that had been done over the past year to 'save the girls from immorality' as Rev. Varney put it. He stressed that the church wanted to get 'the girls away from evil and get them into work of happy usefulness'. The figures showed that during the year, 158 girls and five babies had been admitted to St Monica's. By 1930, St Monica's had been approved by the Ministry of Health as a place of reception for unmarried mothers.

Obviously, poverty had a detrimental effect on health, especially perhaps for those in the local workhouse at Rochford. This institution, which had replaced several smaller units around the Southend area in 1837, did have a static water tank and, by 1858, a nurse (paid more than local schoolmistresses), plus by 1865, a small chapel and vapour and sulphur baths which were particularly good for scabies. Surgical appliances such as wooden legs, trusses and spectacles were issued by the workhouse, and there is a reference to the use, in 1875, of chloroform for the operation on Eliza Hazelton to remove diseased bone from her thigh. In 1891, a padded room was introduced for lunatics and a stomach pump was mentioned 'for treating suicides'.

However, wives were separated from their husbands and children, made to wear uncomfortable clothing, sporting a prominent and debilitating 'P', and confined to barrack-style accommodation. In 1900, one member of the Board of Guardians reported seeing a woman stoking a boiler in the boiler-house, a difficult task for even the toughest of men.

If breaching the rules, women were put on bread and water in solitary confinement, even worse than spending their days oakum picking. In 1907, Catherine Swaffield, having been found drunk in the Royal Stores (public house), had been detained at the workhouse on the hardest laundry work that could be found, with scanty food. When the case came to court, it was revealed that she had been sent to the workhouse because she had tried to commit suicide after being locked up in the police cell in Southend. Mrs Swaffield said she would rather go to prison than return to the workhouse, but was discharged into the care of the Church Army Home at Coleman Row. Generally, however, little information regarding the day-to-day lives of those in the workhouse is available due to a ban on press attendance. This was only lifted when John Burrows, the proprietor of the *Southend Standard*, made the secrecy an issue after being voted in as one of the Guardians in 1886 – he also supported the abolition of workhouse dress for children. Inmates did, at least, have beef with vegetables and plum pudding at Christmas, with a gift of beer and tobacco. From 1881, the workhouse clerk was advertising the boarding-out of pauper children, with expenses paid by the workhouse. Three applications were received, having been offered 3*s* per week board and lodging and 1*s* per week for clothes, school and medical expenses. At a meeting of the Literary Society in November, 1896 (reported in the *Southend Standard*), a Mrs Seel read a paper on Poor Law Reform, and strongly advocated the election of married women to the Board of Guardians as being helpful and useful, a suggestion approved by local Alderman Burrows. Nevertheless, as paupers were eliminated, with the coming of the welfare state, the Rochford Workhouse evolved too, becoming a small hospital, and was eventually handed over to the Southend Public Health Committee in 1930.

For women who escaped the workhouse, and who were not poverty stricken, there certainly seemed to be health benefits of living in Southend. Such benefits were confirmed by such local residents as Mrs Coulson Kernahan (a successful writer who lived in Westcliff-on-Sea) who wrote in *Vogue* magazine in

1897 that she lived in the area by 'deliberate choice' because it was 'Southend-on-Salt-Water, with wonderful changing skies, the quiet of the Hamlet Court Estate, easy accessibility to London and because the air is exactly suited to children.' Others moved to the town specifically for their health, including Mary Buchanan, accompanying her author husband Robert in 1881 after she was diagnosed with cancer, having suffered a range of ailments over the years and become a semi-invalid. Sadly, the move did not prolong her life more than a few months. Until well into the twentieth century, doctors were recommending patients visit or live in Southend 'because of the ozone', with hardstanding constructed across the foreshore to enable visitors to inhale the ozone (a health-giving gas) rising from the mud at low tide.

This was not always necessarily the case, with Mary Braddon's 1865 novel *Only A Clod* referring to the 'concentrated bleakness of perpetual east winds' at Southend, and Jane Austen in *Emma* (1815) giving the following comment to Mr Woodhouse: 'If you must go to the sea, it had better not have been to Southend. Southend is an unhealthy place.' To the east of Southend, around Shoeburyness and Great Wakering, before the mid-1800s, women were particularly susceptible to what was known as Marsh Fever (probably malaria), owing to the foggy and damp conditions, which were eradicated as the area was developed and the land drained. It was actually claimed that farmers living there could outlive not just one, but as many as a dozen wives! Wives of the military had a slight advantage over other local women when a Memorial Hospital for Women was built near to the Shoebury Garrison in 1898, funded by donations from the public, to commemorate all those who had died in a tragic explosion there thirteen years before. (This became a Military Families Hospital, but is now a pub!)

At a meeting at the Co-operative Assembly Room in Southchurch Road in November, 1899, Alderman Thompson from Richmond gave a speech in his role as a pioneer worker 'in the direction of the Municipal Housing of the Working Classes.' The *Southend Standard* quotes him as being 'troubled by the prevalence of infantile mortality at Southend… [when the] borough … was about the healthiest in all England for child life'. He said that 'London doctors recommended the place for young families and with good reason as hundreds had found, and were finding, out. Still the mortality of infant life was great during ten weeks of the summer quarter.' He felt that part of the reason lay in the 'overcrowding of the working-class districts, greatly increased by householders desiring to secure some lodging money wherewith to get through the winter.' Alderman W. Thompson pointed out that 'more would be killed in a slum than in the battles which had already been fought during the war in South Africa'.

While infant mortality was gradually improving in all parts of the UK, the Health Committee of 19 June 1900 discussed an increase in the number of deaths in local babies aged under 1 year. This resulted in the production of a pamphlet 'Advice to Mothers on the Feeding and Care of Infants', to be given to anyone registering a birth. The pamphlet recommended the avoidance of beer and spirits 'while suckling', and stressed that if a substitute for mother's milk was necessary then 'fresh cows' milk delivered by the milkman and boiled immediately' should be used, as boiled milk kept twice as long as unboiled. The 'recipe' was minuted as follows:

> Ingredients: one part cows' milk to three parts thin barley water, plus small lump of white sugar. To make barley water, put two teaspoons pearl barley into one pint of cold water, boil down to 2/3 of a pint and strain through muslin; prepare twice per day and keep in cool place.

Babies born in Rochford Workhouse were particularly vulnerable, with a number of stillborns recorded in the register held at the Essex Record Office. This register also started recording in 1901 whether babies born there were legitimate or illegitimate, and the vast majority were, indeed, illegitimate – e.g. all eleven births in 1902 were illegitimate, although this improved over the years, seven of the thirty-three babies born in 1913 were legitimate (although ten were stillborn), and 125 of the 130 births in 1929 legitimate. Home births were the norm in the nineteenth century, with some interesting cases detailed in the diary of the wife of Dr George Willing who moved to Wakering in 1865. The couple had six children of their own, but Mrs Mary Willing wrote of midwifery cases such as one that took all night in March 1867. Weeks later, Mrs Grace of nearby Barling died in 'child-bed' in spite of Dr Willing's efforts during another long night, leaving a family of nine small children. At this time, of course, there were only the first primitive methods of birth control used – unreliable syringes, tubes, sponges and pessaries. Birth control featured prominently on the agendas of National Council of Women meetings in Southend in the 1920s (as did other subjects such as maternal morbidity). In 1923, the Southend branch passed a resolution urging that birth control advice be given to married women at ante-natal clinics.

Children born into families who were part of the sect of Peculiar People were even more vulnerable, as the sect believed in the power of God to cure all ills rather than in medical intervention. The movement was started in 1838 in Rochford, and babies like 9-month-old Henrietta Eliza Harrod in 1886 died unnecessarily. In Henrietta's case, she had whooping cough for three weeks which was left untreated, resulting in her demise in her 'Lower Southend' home.

As elsewhere, homeopathic medicines and home treatments were popular at the end of the nineteenth century. Local philanthropist, Augusta Tawke, wrote of a Mr Montagu (c. 1860) who was concerned about his housekeeper, in his service for more than half a century. She was told she had diabetes, and did not have long to live, but Mr Montagu dosed her daily with 'a glass of port wine' – for another thirty years! In September, 1873, one advertisement in the *Southend Standard* is for a chemist at Edinburgh Terrace on the Milton Estate, promoting homeopathic cures for children's ailments in particular, and to 'persons suffering from bronchitis or throat disease, who will find speedy relief'. Three choices of cure for smallpox were featured in the *Essex Newsman* of February 1885 – involving either foxglove and zinc which effected a cure 'in a week or less without leaving a mark', or applying 'croton oil and tartaric ointment', or using cream of tartar which cured 'the worst case of smallpox in three days'. What is especially fascinating about the plethora of advertisements for chemists is the outrageous claims that were being made for their goods. Charles King in the High Street, for instance, claimed that the constant use of King's Effervescent Lemon, Lime and Grape Saline kept the blood 'pure' and prevented 'fevers and epidemics' – for just 1*s* 9*d*. Or there was King's Cough Elixir which was a 'certain cure' for coughs, colds, influenza, asthma, shortness of breath or tightness of the chest. In the 1906 recipe book published by the New Congregational Church of Westcliff-on-Sea, there is a cure for erysipelas (a bacterial infection of the skin): put two ounces of ground ivy in a quart of cold water, boil, then simmer for three hours, strain and take a quarter pint hot or cold twice a day.

David Lee published a small booklet in 1975 about his grandparents' fish shop in Leigh in 1905, and writes of his father being rushed to the chemist's nearby after falling and cutting his cheek – the chemist took on the role of doctor and stitched the cut, minor surgery regarded as a common event. There was a similar example in the *Chelmsford Chronicle* of 6 August 1880 when a 'young excursionist' who had fallen down the cliffs and broken her arm in two places was taken to a High Street chemist, where Dr Jones 'set the limb'. However, at the beginning of the twentieth century, the town was still promoting its healthy environment, and was proud of the ladies 'lavatory accommodation' installed in the High Street in 1897. So many people were arriving to take advantage of the healthy air and water, there were bath-chair jams on the cliffs, so much so that in 1907 their use was forbidden after 6 p.m., although special inclines were built to add to the comfort of the occupants. (Bath-chairs could be hired from Wright's Cycle Stores in Richmond Avenue.) In 1908, a report by the local Medical Officer of Health refers to the 'very large amount of light reflected at low tide from the sandy flats', which 'contribute[s] to the efficacy of the place in effecting a cure in cases of consumption and tuberculosis'. The 'extraordinary effect the town had upon ladies who were more or less invalids before they arrived' was part of an early *Standard Guide to Southend*. Leigh-on-Sea was promoting itself similarly, with a 1908 guide describing it as 'pre-eminently a resort for those who are seeking to restore lost health' because of its 'bracing winds from the North Sea and the ozone from its beds when the tide recedes'.

Fundraising and charitable donations were obviously important then, as now, to provide support for the local needy. As early as 1881, a soup kitchen opened in the Mews, off the High Street, serving 2,000 quarts of soup to poverty-stricken families in its first year alone. A soup kitchen was also opened towards the end of the First World War in Shoebury, by the captain of the local fire brigade and his wife; local children were sent there with jugs to be filled. In the *Southend and Westcliff Graphic* during 1912 there are a couple of examples of one class helping another. Miss Bannester and Miss Brown of the Alexandra College arranged a 'magical entertainment' by their pupils to raise money for the United Methodist Church in Leigh Road, who had distributed twenty tons of coal, bread and groceries in the previous year, and had supplied forty-six joints of meat at Christmas, benefiting seventy families. Further, a generous sum of £30,000 was allocated by the will of Sir Lloyd Wise for the establishment of 'homes for necessitous gentlewomen', preferably at Southend, but where this money actually ended up has not been established.

'Gentlewomen' were also catered for before the First World War by a home in Kings Road called the St Ursula's Invalid and Residential Home for Ladies, with several mentions (mainly regarding recruitment of staff) in editions of the *Southend Standard and Essex Weekly Advertiser*. Middle-class Victorian and Edwardian women with mental health issues were for the most part hidden away (as per *Jane Eyre*'s Mrs Rochester), but not necessarily in a home. For instance, William Thackeray's wife, Isabella (on whom he is said to have based the heroine of *Vanity Fair*), who seems to have suffered from extended post-natal depression, was placed under the care of Dr Robert Bakewell, and spent some forty years in Southend, living first with the Bakewells at Whitegate Road and Hadleigh Hall Lodge. When the doctor died, his widow continued to care for Isabella until she moved again to live with Henry Thompson (the organist for Leigh Church) and his wife at Eden Lodge, or Eden House, in Leigh-on-Sea. She lingered on for many years, identifiable by neighbours as always wearing black, visited mainly by her daughter and her doctor, George Deeping. Isabella died aged 77 in 1893 (thirty years after William), and is buried in Leigh Cemetery, London Road, in a plot marked with a Celtic cross. (Psychiatric cases after 1853 had a resource at the Essex County Lunatic Asylum at Warley, near Brentwood, and from 1937 at Runwell, just north of Southend, years after the 1908 County Asylums Act.)

The disabled before and after the turn of the twentieth century had a similarly tough time. Local bestselling novelist of the 1920s onwards, Warwick Deeping, wrote of his childhood in Southend, and refers to a sister born with a hare-lip. Mrs Deeping (wife of the doctor mentioned elsewhere) did not want the disability to be perceived as genetic, so preferred to deny its existence. For working-class families with disabled children, there was help at hand – of a sort. There are some cases archived by the Children's Society – Rachel Dobson, born in Foulness in 1878, is one case. She was born 'paralysed' and her father was too ill to work, so they found Rachel a home in 1897 where she could learn a trade, but it was in Croydon, and was short-lived (though no reason is given for this). Similarly, Irene Whickman, born in Southend in 1901 with a tubercular hip, had poverty-stricken parents who could not afford for her to have special care, and she was sent to a special school, part of an orthopaedic hospital, also in Surrey, in 1914, but again this move only lasted around six months, its termination perhaps being war related.

Men like Rachel's father, breadwinners struck down by illness, had their wages stopped, so, if their wives had large families to look after, institutions such as the Slate Club were initiated. There was one organised by the Brightside Institute at the Clifftown Estate in 1912, and at least one other, at Shopland Mission (north of Southend) by the 1920s. Families would pay in a few pence each week to cover for sickness, with anything left over at Christmas distributed. Some relief also came with the Maternal and Child Welfare Act of 1918, empowering the introduction of day nurseries and health visitors.

But it was the middle-class women of the town who were the backbone of fundraising, with their biggest efforts towards the end of the nineteenth century centred around getting a local hospital off the ground. (There had been a military hospital from 1856 attached to Shoebury barracks, later a 'military families' hospital'.) Although Lady Brooke, the future Countess of Warwick, laid the foundation stone for the first hospital in Warrior Square in August 1887, fundraising had started a year earlier with a large-scale bazaar thanks to a committee of ladies, supported by local doctors who felt the time had come for the town to have its own cottage hospital. Opening in May 1888, the Victoria Hospital needed the Ladies' Hospital Working Party to keep it going from 1891, as the number of patients increased from 61 in 1889 to 601 in 1908. This cottage hospital, interestingly, had rules barring patients with infectious diseases, advanced consumption, incurable or chronic diseases or were of 'unsound mind or in an advanced stage of pregnancy'! Princess Louise commemorated the fundraising efforts involved in establishing the hospital by unveiling a plaque on 4 December 1912.

As for infectious diseases, treatment in Southend was based at the sanitary hospital in Prittlewell Street from c.1890, moving to Balmoral Road in 1895, patients arriving at the hospital via 'hand-litter', these patients paying between 2*s* and 2 guineas per week. Before this, local doctors were treating male and female patients with cholera, for example, at home, exposing themselves to risk. Philip Benton's history of the area published in 1888 refers to how diseases such as scarlet fever devastated families; in 1863, for example, the rector of Rochford lost two daughters: Edith age 5 and Nora aged just 1, together with two nieces, Elizabeth, aged 10, and Eva, 3. In 1860 in *Letters from*

Leigh, the King family wrote of smallpox injections, of malaria treated with quinine, and of the use of mustard plasters and linseed poultices. Six years later, these letters refer to the high number of cholera deaths in Leigh – as many as sixty-four in one week alone, mainly 'south of the railway' (i.e. in the poorer area, dominated by the fishing fraternity), and perhaps partly due to the nearest doctor being in Prittlewell, some miles away. There are cases of typhoid and scarlet fever mentioned in 1887, with whooping cough and consumption featuring in some 1888 letters.

Typhoid also features regularly in the reports of the local Medical Officer (or, variously, Inspector) of Health. On 6 August 1880, a Dr Thorne is quoted in the *Chelmsford Chronicle*, he explains that it is Prittlewell and not Southend (Prittlewell being just north of Southend) that has 'wholly neglected' sanitary conditions, with 100 cases in that area between September 1879 and February 1880, although the population was then just 600. He described the wells, cesspools and privy-pits as in 'direct communication', especially after heavy rainfall, leading to an 'exceptionally polluted state'. He recommended the local authority 'to amend as quickly as possible the sanitary condition of the village', which would otherwise lead to a risk of Southend town being damaged as 'by extension of buildings … [Prittlewell] appears to be about to become a part of the town'. However, in another of his reports in 1902, he describes Southend as 'an endemic centre' for the disease, the main causes being the inadequate sewerage and the local preference for burying untreated excreta in gardens. Cockles that were laid down in sewage-polluted creeks were recommended for closure, with eleven of thirteen cases of typhoid that year having been shellfish eaters. Also in that year, although there were four cases of smallpox (also called variola) in Southend, the Health Committee reported that recently-introduced vaccinations were making a big difference (vaccinations against smallpox were compulsory from 1853). The same committee became involved in discussing Mrs Selkirk who had exposed 'a child suffering from diptheria in a public place without proper protection against spreading the disease' in 1904. They decided to send a letter threatening proceedings if the offence was repeated, which seemed to work. (School absenteeism was more likely to be from measles, or what is described in the Hinguar School log book in 1901, for instance, as 'bad heads', 'bad hands', or even St Vitus Dance.)

The local minutes reveal a growing awareness of health hazards – in 1910, the local Master Bakers' Association was concerned about the undesirable sale of stale bread, and the local authority was to take measures for the destruction of all rats to prevent disease. By February 1911, no incidences of typhoid had been reported for twelve months. (Other diseases took longer to dissipate: diptheria, for instance, did not disappear until the 1940s.) There is a later case – in the *Southend and Westcliff Graphic* of 5 February 1915 – of a nurse contracting scarlet fever.

Such diseases were the most common cause of death for Victorians, with heart failure also often caused by rheumatic fever. Cancer was relatively rare, but, for women, death in childbirth was common (often due to infection), as was death from burns. The latter can be attributed to open fires, open-hearth cooking and highly flammable fabrics. Nurse Ellen Daly was one of those who set her clothes alight while cooking – in her case, for patients at Southend Sanatorium in March 1915. Although she was severely burned, she put out the flames unaided, and carried on with her duties but collapsed and died from her injuries and shock a few hours later. Diseases such as Parkinson's Disease were not generally recognised even into the early 1920s, at a time when any mysterious symptoms were dismissed as having been picked up 'in the trenches' and passed on. Although strokes also caused death, these were associated with middle and upper classes who ate more animal food and less fruit and vegetables than the poor. The *Southend and Westcliff Graphic* of 3 August 1917 recommended that women grow medicinal herbs as it was 'not too strenuous, an intellectual study, a means of pecuniary profit and a patriot stimulus'.

During the First World War, the Palace Hotel on Southend seafront (now the Park Inn Palace) was transformed into HM Queen Mary's Royal Naval Hospital with its first intake in October 1914, when 168 Belgian soldiers arrived by train, with wounded soldiers from the British Expeditionary Force following soon after, including casualties from Ypres. By March 1917, over 4,000 British soldiers and sailors had been treated, although only sailors were admitted after that date. This hospital was mainly staffed by nurses from the Voluntary Aid Detachment (VADs). It seems to have had one of the first made-to-measure X-ray departments in the country, if not in the world – although at this stage there was no protection for staff. The Glen in Southchurch Road, previously a holiday home, was converted into a wartime hospital by the local branch of the Red Cross, as was the Overcliff Hotel on The Leas. The hospital in Warrior Square did continue to serve local residents, however.

Post war, Mrs Henry White formed the Southend Victoria Hospital Auxiliary Fund Committee, having already organised the Hospital Saturday Workers. The ladies concerned had raised money during the war for the Glen and Overcliff hospitals. A Wednesday Working Party was formed by Mrs Dowdy in 1920, these ladies meeting up at the hospital to repair linen. After HRH the Duchess of York (later Queen Elizabeth, the Queen Mother) laid the foundation stone of Southend's brand new hospital in Prittlewell Chase in November 1929, fundraising continued, with the Ladies Working Party still just as important, as was the Ladies Linen League who produced 5,000 articles in 1934 alone.

The first ante-natal clinic locally opened on 5 May 1920 in Westcliff. Maternity cases were mainly handled at Rochford Hospital, originally the workhouse infirmary, which had expanded by the 1920s to include a new block for 'feeble-minded' patients. It increased the number of maternity beds from thirty in 1939 to ninety in 1946. The Public Health Act of 1936 helped expectant mothers by introducing home helps, activated locally in 1938. The infant-mortality rate had improved by 1943 (to 33 per 1,000 births) but the maternity death rate was a little higher than the rest of the country, at more than 3 per 1,000 births, these figures perhaps distorted by wartime displacement. In 1946, the Secretary of the Southend-on-Sea District Business and Professional Women's Club, Miss Barbara Chippindale, sent a letter to local MPs urging the government to issue a form of birth certificate for general purposes which did not disclose that a person was illegitimate – nice thought and nice try, but unsuccessful.

Two lady doctors who had specialised in eye disease in London hospitals established the South East Essex Eye Hospital in London Road in 1930, again thanks to voluntary contributions, but this was replaced by the better equipped new general hospital from 1932. The health of local women (and men, come to that) was looking up, but women were to be foregrounded locally when, also in 1932, the Women's League of Health and Beauty opened a local branch. This newly developing organisation was aware of the benefits to women of exercise – and, indeed, of more relaxed clothing – and classes were also designed to be sociable, benefiting the many recently bereaved.

The need for volunteers in Southend's hospitals continued. In fact, the Commandant of the Southend Red Cross, Miss C. Robinson, was reported in the *Southend Standard* of 2 June 1949 as saying that in the last year 'her members, nearly all of whom are housewives or businesswomen, did 2,728 hours duty in their spare time at the hospital and health centre.' The Red Cross was still self-funded, and, despite the introduction of the National Health Service, was still in need of flag days etc.

CHAPTER FIVE

Leisure

While leisure pursuits for Southend women changed – as for everyone – with the advances of literacy and technology, and with slow improvements financially for those at the bottom of the income ladder, they were also influenced by the growth of the population and the input of its women. However, this is not to say that Victorian women did not know how to enjoy themselves. The Prittlewell Fair, held annually in the nineteenth century, is an example of the pleasure that could be derived for a little money. There were shows on Goodman's Green (then south of East Street) featuring dwarves, 'giants' and such joys as a 'learned pig', stalls in North Street and West Street selling gooseberry pie and potatoes plus sausages for a penny and bread for a halfpenny, games and cart races, a booth outside The Eagle for dancers and other local pubs open for most of the day. Sadly, spoilsport Lord of the Manor of Prittlewell Priory, Daniel Scratton, complained in 1872 that it caused immorality and injuries. Fairs generally were regarded as a social evil in many quarters, not just locally. Mr Scratton organised a petition to close the local fair, also signed by local shopkeepers and luminaries including the Lord of the Manor of nearby Earls Hall, and so it was indeed abolished.

Happily, before the demise of the fair, a Public Hall had opened in Alexandra Street in Southend's town centre, a much needed facility for entertainment and meetings from 1870. It changed its name to the Empire Theatre and, although destroyed by fire in 1895, was rebuilt and survived in various guises until the twenty-first century. In 1873, it staged the first production of the Royal Alexandra Dramatic Company – 'Lady Audley's Secret' – which was followed by 'a most laughable negro farce,' plus Miss Maud Ranford of Opera Bouffe and Miss Mervyn of the Theatre Royal, Drury Lane 'specially engaged for this occasion'. The *Southend Standard* in October that year refers to this company as needing two ladies to fill up the cast for the second entertainment to be given in November, with professional instruction to be provided 'gratis' in elocution and acting. Not all the male population were that keen on their wives participating in amateur dramatics, as featured in the *Southend Standard* of 6 March 1924 – a production of La Mascotte from Southend's Operatic and Dramatic Society (formed c.1892) had its leading lady 'removed from rehearsals' by her husband! Music hall was particularly popular at the beginning of the twentieth century, although when the Hippodrome in Southchurch Road opened in 1908 the unexpected photographer's flashlight reduced some of the women in the audience to screams. This theatre and the Pier Pavilion in particular attracted well-known stars of the period including Vesta Tilley and Marie Lloyd at the Hippodrome, and one of the Gibson girls, Camille Clifford, on the pier in 1906. The *Southend Standard* critic seems to have been overawed by her costume, 'which I have not the temerity to describe'. There was also a 'Prince's Hall of Varieties' in Tylers Avenue, advertising in local papers in 1908. Even more affordable was the Floral Hall on the seafront at Westcliff – where lady residents and visitors could just enjoy the music at the bandstand on the cliffs for free. The Palace Theatre opened in 1912, and attracted such big names as Mrs Patrick Campbell. By the 1930s, Southend had its own theatrical costumier in Hamlet Court Road, known as Madam Norman.

A roller rink in Alexandra Street also proved popular with local womenfolk when it opened in 1876 – complete with bandstand, aviaries, fountains and rock gardens. The class divide here meant that those who could afford roller-skates could join in the fun, seemingly unhampered by flowing skirts, while others could just watch, as it was an open air venue. Those preferring ice-skating, and with a few pence to spare, could wait for the lake in Southend Park (its five acres long gone) to freeze over, this park offering cycle racing from c.1875 plus cricket, croquet, tennis, fishing, athletics, gymnastics, with an annual firework display. Note that fishing was not a one-sex sport; for instance, at the first Sea Angling Festival in 1904, 'many of the fairer sex turned out with rod and line', according to the *Southend Standard.* The same newspaper on 20 June 1907 mentions a monthly meeting of the Southend Angling Society held at the Middleton Hotel, with a 'large attendance of ladies and gentlemen'. There is a British Pathé film available online, dated 1929, featuring two middle-aged women fishing with rods from the end of the pier, with a close up of another woman's hands baiting her hook with a maggot and other smiling women holding up rods with fish on the end.

A reading room at the established Marine Library near the foot of Pier Hill was opened in 1875, a location where Old and New Southend met which was frequented (according to Miss Tawke in her *Hunting Recollections* of 1913) by the fashionable of the day, with even a facility for either buying 'Berlin wool' to make cushions or cotton for tatting. This library was replaced in 1906 by premises in Victoria Avenue which boasted a Ladies' Room – now Southend Central Museum. (By 1951, there were libraries in Leigh-on-Sea, Southchurch, Westcliff and Rochford, with one at Shoeburyness on land sold in 1934 to Southend Corporation 'for a nominal sum' by Miss Knapping, Lady of the Manor.) In the *Southend Standard* of 22 September 1927, there is a detailed account of 'What Women Read'. The head librarian in Southend said that 'good use was made' of works on 'domestic science, dressmaking and kindred subjects'. He also felt that poorer folk wanted to read about society, while those 'fairly well placed' wanted to read about the slums (!) with women particularly interested in historical novels. Women were also influenced, it seems, by reviews in the press, with an average of two novels read each week by female clients, and they were regarded as not only bigger borrowers, but as bigger book-buyers than men. The *Southend Times* of 24 February 1931 makes a distinction for 'young women' readers who apparently preferred books about botany and animals.

Southend's famous pier, a popular tourist destination since its first primitive wooden format in the 1830s (but extended and improved over the years), was offering little more than a penny photo machine 'popular with the ladies' by 1892. Predictably, perhaps, complaints were made to the Pier Committee about 'the nature and titles' of the pictures being exhibited in the Mutoscopes on the pier in 1901 (e.g. What The Butler Saw). From 1898 to 1905, there was an added attraction on the seafront: the Warwick Revolving Tower which councillors' wives were too scared to go up in – partly the height (150ft) with views at the top that made them nervous, and partly the fact that it acquired a reputation for breaking down.

Marine Park (Old Southend), close to the shoreline, was popular from 1894 for local sporting events including a trotting track, but the area evolved into the Kursaal Amusement Park with its pleasure gardens of some 26 acres in 1901, featuring the world's first lady lion tamer! (It also featured the first female wall-of-death rider, Marjorie Ward, in 1929.) Less happily, a nurse from East Ham, Miss Ellen Smith, fell to her death in July 1921 from the Harton Scenic Railway, although this did not seem to deter visitors. During the Second World War, the Kursaal's dance hall closed, but dances were held elsewhere in the town, even though local ladies had to contend with partners in heavy boots, carrying gas masks and tin hats. Later, the Kursaal's sprung floor ballroom experienced the progression from old-time dances to jive, causing the whole building to vibrate and the mirror ball to swing alarmingly. (In the 1950s, the introduction of stilettos meant that the floor eventually had to be replaced.)

By 1913, the High Street had become a very busy centre, with a good variety of shops; with the town now offering green spaces, gardens, trams (which replaced privately owned horse-drawn omnibuses), hotels, inns and cinemas. The 3*d* charge to stroll through the Shrubbery fronting Royal Terrace was apparently dropped around this time, its green-coated guardians having been a means of keeping the lower classes away from the rich families in the Terrace!

Bathing, to take advantage of the perceived health benefits, had been popular with residents and visitors since the eighteenth century, with a spa just a few miles away at Hockley, which had been built on the site of a 'medicinal' spring in 1842. On the seafront at Southend, floating swimming baths were established in the nineteenth century, moored off Western Esplanade (until the First World War). A complaint was sent to the local board by the Rev. Thackeray in August 1884 objecting to boys and girls bathing together in the harbour, which he described as 'disgraceful'. This particular issue continued into the twentieth century, with the local board proposing in 1912 that no male should be allowed within 25yds of a female bather. Bathing – or changing – machines had been introduced before this to protect female modesty, and lady 'dippers' were employed to hold customers in their arms and dip them in the waters before returning them to the changing machines. There were ten such machines – some pulled by horses, others by a winding mechanism – at the foot of Pier Hill as well as others on the Esplanades either side of the pier. Dippers were the robust wives of local fishermen, bearing in mind that most of those being dipped could not swim. There were a few exceptions: one was a heroic young woman who, in September 1856, plunged into the waves to rescue her brother and an elderly man with cramp that he was trying to help, managing to get them both into a boat brought to assist by another brother – the young woman, Emma Ingram, was described in the *Chelmsford Chronicle* as another 'Grace Darling'. Another was visitor Nelly Power, appearing at London's Vaudeville Theatre in 1872, who was bathing at the same time as an un-named girl of 'about 12 or 13 years' who kept disappearing beneath the waves, perhaps with tiredness. Nelly managed to bring her ashore, to the hearty cheers of spectators. One woman at Leigh who hired a bathing machine in 1917 drowned, resulting in a fine for the owner who had not provided an emergency rowing boat as obliged by his licence.

The Pier Committee of 1895 proposed that the new seawater baths near the pier entrance known as the 'Cleopatra Baths' be divided to provide separate entrances for men and women, which was agreed. Council minutes of 1898 refer to the prohibiting of bathing between 6 a.m. and 9 p.m. except from a bathing machine, and these machines were licensed annually. Demand for them fell when men and women could inhabit the same beach and with the opening of Westcliff swimming pool in 1915, but the law regarding changing was not repealed until the 1940s, with machines still in use in the 1930s.

One female activity that has disappeared locally since the Victorian era is the sport of hunting. In Philip Benton's nineteenth-century *History of the Rochford Hundred*, he refers to a Mrs and Miss Rankin being among those joining in the local hunt in 1877, although it was more usual for ladies to follow the hunt on foot, bravely jumping across ditches, picking their way through the fields of mangolds and dashing through woods and hedges in their long skirts. Benton also gave pigeon shooting parties in the 1860s, attended by such as Mrs Willing, the doctor's wife from Wakering, and Miss Tawke, who wrote of shooting competitions attended, on Eastern Esplanade, by 'the grandees of the County'. In her *Hunting Recollections* of 1911 she refers to ladies being 'generally first in a run in the hunting field', and, 'it is great to see our leading lady pop over a gate or stile'. Even the farmer's daughter, she felt, had plenty of fun 'on a steady old cob', with 'the quiet lady rider, always calm and collected, affording a striking contrast' to those whose language was 'a trifle warm'. She quoted one particular rider who had been told to mind the drop in front of her, but had responded with 'D … the drop.' (Warm language indeed!) Two able riders mid-nineteenth century were the daughters of Leigh fisherman Isaac Partridge, who left Leigh Old Town and married into a new life as part of an equestrian circus troupe. (This information the result of Councillor Carole Mulroney's research as a member of the Leigh Society.)

Before the age of the motor car, cycling was very popular with Southend women who could afford to either buy or hire a bicycle.

In fact, there was a local cycling club in situ by 1890, with penny farthings featuring until the 1920s. Mr Wright of Wright's Cycle Stores taught ladies and gents how to cycle during the summer season. In *Derbyshire's Guide to Southend-on-Sea* (1901), there are details of the Southend-on-Sea Cycle Club headquarters at the Alexandra Hotel. The Royal Hotel was the headquarters of the Cyclists' Touring Club, promoting a book of female cycle circuits available for just 1*d.* In 1907, the *Southend Standard and Essex Weekly Advertiser* mentions the 'latest fad' seen in the High Street, this being a 'lady cycling with her pet dog in an open dress hamper on a carrier arrangement in front'. In the 1920s, holiday guides featured bicycles made for two and also reminded readers that cycling was cheaper than the train.

The tedium of many women's lives was broken by feast days such as May Day or Bonfire Night, with attractions such as Morris dancers. For those tied to home, or who were not particularly 'sporty', there were specific sedentary interests available. Mrs Willing, whose 1865–67 diaries are mentioned elsewhere, wrote of playing vingt-et-un and other card games, of sewing clothes for the children, and attending 'Penny Readings' of the classics. Outdoors, time was spent bringing home crabs from the beach, bathing, sailing, fishing, gardening and picnics. At Christmas, this particular family was able to enjoy visits from singers and mummers, and a spread of goose and spiced beef.

Predictably, many Victorian women's lives revolved around the church, although many were also tied to the family fireside and a plethora of children, unless they could afford a nanny. Sunday observance was often perceived to cure the evil of immorality, and women were encouraged to lead bible classes for ladies and girls, or to help in the Sunday school. It was the women, of course, who also took on the responsibility for flowers in the churches, especially at harvest time. Local churches were behind a number of groups of mothers who met up regularly. In June 1891, the Rev. Varney of All Saints Church in Sutton Road was presented with a clock and inkstand by a group of these mothers, in appreciation of his kindness and the interest he had taken in them. The meetings were held weekly in the 'Parish Room, Porters Town', and Rev. Varney thanked the many mothers present, 'for it showed they appreciated what efforts had been made on their behalf'. He also pointed out that he had been told that 'poor people were never grateful for what was done for them', but he personally had never 'found it lacking among the poor when work for them had been carried out in a right spirit'. Families in rural areas outside Southend would walk miles to church, often making a day of it by taking a packed lunch with them.

Church could also be a social centre. The Wesleyan Methodist Church sisterhood, then in York Road, arranged charabanc outings and weekly meetings with female speakers and female soloists. A quote from their newsletter in November 1927 notes that 'all ladies not attached to another women's meeting are assured of a warm welcome at York Road', and that their Thrift Club was open to all. St Saviour's Church in Kings Road, Westcliff, also had a Thrift Club for canny savers in the 1930s. St Mary's in Prittlewell arranged dances for people 'to meet in healthy recreation, and also to encourage and foster the family spirit in our parochial life' – a quote from their 1933 parish magazine. They also held Mothers' Union meetings, with unmarried women eligible for 'associated membership'. By that time, the Avenue Baptist Church in Westcliff had established a Girls' Life Brigade, a sewing group, a Young Women's Association including a Bible class, and a Women's Happy Hour. St Luke's ran a Women's Fellowship with speakers on 'Labour Saving and Money Saving in the Home', 'The Care of Children in Sickness and in Health', 'New Clothes from Old', and 'Curing Rabbit Skins'. By 1947, Leigh's Wesley Methodist Church had a Women's Club, a Young Wives' Club, and had arranged concerts for their dramatic society featuring local talented sisters Peggy (comedienne of later television fame) and Nancy Mount (pianist).

Many sports, previously perceived as unfeminine, thrived as clothing became more relaxed and the benefits of exercise began to be understood. There is a reference in *Letters from Leigh* to a ladies' cricket match in 1884 at Shoebury Garrison, with Canon King's daughter, Emmie, scoring eleven not out in the first innings. An early reference to women golfers is in 1907 when Rochford Hundred Golf Club boasted a Ladies Club. In 1908, a year after its opening, Thorpe Hall Golf Club in Thorpe Bay had 40 lady members of the 291 total membership. This club had its first lady captain c. 1914 in Hester Ormsby-Cooke who moved into the club house with her husband when she heard reports of a possible military takeover by the army; she kitted herself out in farming overalls and bought a flock of geese so that when the soldiers arrived, she could claim that the land was a farm, and the officer in charge apologised for their 'mistake'. The *Essex Chronicle* of 2 May 1930 refers to Mrs Percy Garon (Garon being a famous name at the time, with a whole chain of shops and restaurants in Southend from the 1890s) winning her fourth successive Essex Women's Golf Championship at the Rochford Hundred golf course. A short history of Thorpe Hall Golf Club written in 1931 mentions the 'ladies' charming quarters'.

Hockey is mentioned in the Entertainments and Parks Committee minutes in December 1913 when it recommended the use of a hockey pitch at Chalkwell Park, the location for annual hockey festivals after the Second World War. When the Westcliff Tennis Club was formed in 1907, it became remarkable for the success of its lady players. In the 1920s, women were not even averse to taking part in the mud-fights which were part of the annual Leigh Regatta.

There are a number of examples of Southend women who broke the mould, becoming proficient in a range of sports. One of the families (via ancestry.com) has a story of local resident Mabel Read who was a prizewinning fencer before the First World War. Between wars, would-be Channel swimmers were believed to have trained in Southend, including Eva Coleman from London, who apparently set up a few records (un-evidenced). The un-named winner of the first women's 100 yd race in Priory Park in 1925 apparently caused some controversy with her divided skirt (!) but, undeterred, women were taking part in cross-country races as part of the Southend Harriers by 1929, twenty-four years after its formation. In 1933, local girl Dora Greenwood broke the Women's High Jump World Record with 1.65m, losing the record six years later to another Essex girl (Dorothy Odam from Brentwood). Two years later, an alumni of Chalkwell School (Freda James) was one half of the winning Wimbledon Women's Doubles, and repeated her success the following year.

Very different roles were evolving from 1908 with the first appearance of beauty contestants, Southend claiming (no doubt proudly) to be the first town to introduce the seaside beauty competition. This first competition was featured in the *Southend and Westcliff Graphic* of 21 August, using the language of the age – referring to one contestant (from Senegal) as a 'woman of colour', who was apparently a royal princess and whose beauty tip was to bury herself up to her neck in sand every morning. When a poster of bathing beauties appeared in the town in November 1913, advertising the revue 'Splash Me' at the Hippodrome, local Reverend Dormer Pierce denounced the performance, describing it as 'objectionable'. The chorus girls involved called on the Reverend at the vicarage to ask what he meant by 'suggesting suggestiveness'! They alleged that he cast a 'reflection on their morality' (according to the *Essex Newsman* of 22 November). The writer felt that Rev. Pierce had been more than equal to the occasion, claiming that he had not condemned the performance, only the poster. The mayor got involved at this point, mentioning another poster with a lady in corsets which he thought was 'just as bad', but the vicar had not seen this – he vowed, however, to see the revue before the week was out. What he thought of it is not recorded ….

The town's first carnival queen, twenty-two years after the start of the annual carnival, was Ena Bone in 1928, crowned at the Floral Hall on Western Esplanade. Ten years later, this 'advance' in the admiration of the female form was shown by the MP for South East Essex, Victor Raikes, in the *Daily Mirror,* when he announced that he would provide as many 'charming young ladies as I can find to drive cars to bring people to the polls'. The 1930s was the decade featured in a story about a

Yorkshire soldier serving abroad who had heard, similarly, that Southend had an outstanding number of attractive and eligible women and who had written to the mayor in an attempt to find a suitable wife, prompting hundreds of others to copy him once the story broke, until the Council tired of being a one-stop dating agency! (This feature appears in *The Southend Story*). Another possibly retrograde step, not appreciated by the move for equality, was the introduction of nude reviews after the Second World War, which continued – at the Regal in Tylers Avenue – after 1950. Times were certainly a-changin'.

CHAPTER SIX

'Active' Women

While Southend was not an epicentre for the struggle for women's rights, that is not to say that local women did not take an interest. London is only forty miles from Southend, and this was, of course, one of the main hubs of the suffrage movement, along with Manchester. It is important to remember that press coverage during the suffrage period was male-led, there were hardly any female journalists, and that there was a lot else going on including war at home and overseas, so the struggle for the cause did not take priority in local news. However, there are references to the use of stones from Southend's beaches being taken to London in suitcases to serve as weapons for the more violent suffragettes!

In Southend, and especially in the nineteenth century, women were more passive than their famous counterparts in the big cities. Middle-class women, nevertheless, would have been aware of the mouthpiece of feminism commencing publication in 1857 (*The Englishwoman's Journal*); of the unfair Matrimonial Causes Act the same year which denied a wife (not a husband) the means to divorce on grounds of adultery alone; of the beginnings of organised campaigns for women's suffrage, and of the first (defeated) Women's Suffrage Bill in 1870. At this time however, the local press and local journalists were still focusing on the more familiar female role. When Queen Victoria's daughter, Princess Louise, stayed in Southend with her husband (the Duke of Argyll) in 1873, the newspapers were only interested in reporting her accompanying her husband to the military ranges at Shoebury, or her visits to the local jewellers and nurseries (garden centres), rather than presenting her as the advocate of female education and suffrage that she was.

Other press references to local women at the end of the nineteenth century were more focused on their contribution to the local community – as when Mrs Scott, the wife of the proprietor of the Royal Hotel, died in 1869, resulting in many shops closing for the day out of respect. The respect was for her 'contributions for the collections for good or charitable purposes', and her kindness 'to the poor and their families'. Likewise when Miss Heygate (whose brother had been Lord Mayor of London) died in 1879, the *Southend and Essex Weekly Advertiser* pointed out how she was 'beloved by a host of relations and friends, to whom her house was always open, and by the poor, to whom she was most liberal'. There was also a passing reference to her involvement in the origins of the pier. Similarly, Lady Olivia Sparrow, who inherited land in Leigh and Hadleigh from her husband, may not have even lived in the area (although she was known to ride locally, having had local stables and a hunting lodge built for her own use), but in the 1850s donated land for schools, provided wells for a local water supply, and cottages nearby for the poor.

A more detailed account of local involvement was with regard to a meeting held in Rochford in January 1882, debating 'The Extension of Women's Rights', with fifty people in attendance, mostly women, though with a male chair and all male speakers. On the one hand, it was argued that women 'who possess the qualifications which entitle men to vote' should have the right to vote, while on the other hand, 'the political responsibilities of women ought not to be enlarged'. While the women present were asked to speak, no one stepped forward, so the second argument was 'carried' by the all-male vote, the first argument having been proposed apparently only 'for the sake of getting up an argument'! This was not the view of Mrs Brooks, speaking at a meeting of the Southend and District Women's Liberal Association in November 1891. While stressing that the most important feature of the Women's Associations was the educational power they possessed, she also did not agree with the feeling that 'it was unwomanly to take an interest in politics'. She held that her 'womanhood' demanded that she should take an interest in the 'sorrows and sufferings and hardships and grievances' of those among whom she lived; to 'see that wrongs should be righted and mistakes remedied', and she considered that she would fail in her duty if she left 'any stone unturned', until she got those things remedied. This was met with hearty applause.

The town had a visit from Millicent Fawcett in 1892, the woman who, in 1866 when just 19, had organised signatures for the first petition for women's suffrage, although she was too young to sign it herself. She spoke at length at Clarence Hall in Clarence Street on the subject of Women's Suffrage, presided over by Major Rasch MP, who had invited her to attend. He introduced her by saying that 'the parliamentary curtain would rise in a few hours and he would ballot for the bill Mrs Fawcett would explain to them'. (This bill was Sir Algernon Borthwick's Bill to extend the Parliamentary franchise to women.) The *Southend Standard and Essex Weekly Advertiser* described her address as being 'forcible, well-reasoned and splendidly delivered'. She wanted to apply 'the good old constitutional maxim of no taxation, no representation'. Pointing out that,

> nearly every man, however ignorant, who cared to have a vote could get it if he were able to get a house of any sort over his head. Even paupers out of the workhouse could vote if their names had been retained on the parliamentary register, a lunatic could vote in a lucid interval, and a felon just out of gaol also had the advantage of the franchise. Look at the position of about twenty thousand women farmers. Their shepherds, their carters, their ploughmen, their coachmen, their gardeners and their butlers have got a vote, but the women who employ them have not.

She denied that 'women's suffrage could cause women to neglect their domestic duties', and felt it was,

> a very good thing to have the presence of a lady on a School Board ... not the mannish woman, but the womanly woman of gentle manners, good voice, with consideration and sympathy in her manners; in a word, ladies. They did not want in politics women who were bad imitations of men with billycock hats [bowlers] and stick-up collars, loud voices and rough manners,

drawing laughter as well as applause from her audience. She requested that the chairman sign a petition to the House of Commons in support of the Bill and on behalf of the meeting, a motion seconded by Mrs Seal, who said that she 'held herself to be in no way inferior to a man but had no wish to wear her husband's clothes', leading to more laughter and applause. The resolution was carried. (Fawcett was the woman who in 1897 became the president of the National Union of Women's Suffrage Societies, the NUWSS, an amalgam of around seventeen societies in Britain in favour of suffrage.)

It seems that at least one member of the King family from Leigh – i.e., Canon King's 30-year-old daughter, Judy – was following the suffragette movement with interest. She went to a debate in August 1889 in London on Women's Suffrage with male and female speakers, and reported back to her mother that one female speaker had said to one of the male speakers, who was against the suffrage 'Why are you so afraid of us? We would not do you any harm!' This apparently resulted in a 'roar of laughter' all over the room.

There was an awareness in the town of the escalation of the suffrage movement, with the local technical school having taken part in a lengthy debate in 1907, with girls dressed up as suffragettes bearing flags proclaiming: 'Votes for Women'. This is reported in the *Southend Standard and Essex Weekly Advertiser* of 24 December, with some emphasis on the humour – eight girls took on the role of believers, including: 'Miss Isabel Pankake' and 'Lord Fitzherbert Keyblack', with eight in opposition including: 'Farmer Clodhop Giles' and a Cockney 'Bill George Brown'. The girls certainly came up with some original arguments: 'They laughed at the Oriental and Chinese who bound their feet but it was a worse evil, cramping the minds of women', opposed by: 'If women got the vote, what class would they get in Parliament? The quiet educated class or the noisy, boisterous and addle-headed class? The result would be the downfall of Parliament.'

When staunch Liberal, Lady Cecilia Roberts, visited the town in April 1907 (to talk to the Southend and Westcliff Women's Liberal Association), she was aware that the Liberal MP for South East Essex, Rowland Whitehead, was opposed to women's suffrage, placing local women in a 'peculiar' position. According to the reporter in the *Southend Standard and Essex Weekly Advertiser* of 2 May, Lady Cecilia urged her audience to try and convince him and make him realise that women were fit to 'have the suffrage'. She did not believe in unconstitutional methods of violence. ('Hear, hear.') She would rather women did not have the vote than they should do anything unwomanly. ('Applause.') She believed, however, they would get women's suffrage by quiet and constitutional methods. ('Hear, hear.')

The debate continued the following year when, in January, the Southend Liberal Association had a meeting on Women's Suffrage, with local spokeswoman Mrs Osborn doing most of the talking. She pointed out that women had entered 'nearly every occupation and profession, and thousands earned their own living side by side with men and were obliged to pay taxes and income on property, yet were denied the Parliamentary vote'. Her argument was that 'opponents ignored the fact that for forty years the advance guard of women thinkers had been pressing for this reform … [with] bills or resolutions in Parliament brought forward almost every year since 1870 [with] politicians governed by expediency rather than right.' While she conceded the one 'great objection raised … that women could not fight', she also felt strongly that 'in war time very few men comparatively did fight and after all the great war force was money, and women helped pay for war in money and the lives of those dear to them'. Her argument closed with the point that 'while women were received enthusiastically at election times by politicians to do much of the drudgery of election work, yet they must not aspire to enter a polling booth and mark a paper'. The *Southend Standard and Essex Weekly Advertiser* of 23 January 1908 carries a full account of this debate. This is also the date of a postcard held at the Women's Library in London depicting seven women outside Southend Central station wearing Women's Social and Political Union (WSPU) billboards, selling the *Votes for Women* paper – but the image is not of publishable quality unfortunately. Also unfortunate is the lack of evidence to support stories in local newspapers when Leigh-based Florence Reeve passed away in 2005 aged 111, suggesting she had been a young suffragette prior to the First World War, and then joined the WRAF aged 17 as a mess steward.

The author and philanthropist Augusta Saumerez Tawke, mentioned elsewhere, was more focused on helping local women than in joining the suffragettes it seems, in continuance of her mother's work in the nineteenth century. She was chairwoman of the Hockley Parish Council and involved in the erection of a Public Hall in that area which could be used by the WI, of which she was president as well as being president of her local Women's Legion. Then there was her role as chairman of the Rochford and Hockley Nursing Association, Poppy Day organiser, Church Warden, committee member of the Essex Women's War Agricultural Association, chairwoman of the Conservative Association and Governor of Hockley and Hawkwell schools, eventually becoming a local parish councillor. She and her mother were behind the Hockley laundry which taught local unemployed women a trade before the First World War, and she was also behind the teaching of milking at Hockley using an artificial cow. As a gifted artist and wood-carver (as well as a horsewoman), she oversaw the making of teddy bears and toys, especially mechanical toys, with the *Southend and Westcliff Graphic* supporting her efforts with comments such as: 'No need to go to Germany for your toys'! She never married but devoted her life to local 'good works', including fundraising for a new peal of bells at Rochford Church, and, latterly, to the care of the man who had donated the land in Hockley used for that Public Hall. This was one busy role model for the women of Southend until her death in 1947.

In the meantime, local interest in the suffragette movement had grown, initiating a debate by the Leigh Debating Society on 'Women's Suffrage' at Hillside Hall in October 1909, the first time women had been admitted to the society. The *Southend Standard and Essex Weekly Advertiser* pointed out that all the front seats had been taken by local women, with those men in attendance having to stand at the back of the hall. The speaker was Mrs Kineton Parkes, whose home in London became the Headquarters of the Women's Tax Resistance League (WTRL) the following year. She was the first female to open discussions by the society, and proposed that 'the time has now arrived when the Parliamentary franchise should be extended to women on the same terms as now possessed by men'. She said she represented the Women's Freedom League who believed that 'their methods and tactics might be as militant as they liked, but they did not care how militant they were'. She remarked that she 'had been a frightfully respectable person, Vice-President of a Women's Liberal Association', but felt they ought to go further, especially after visiting some of the leaders of the movement and listening to their arguments. Plus, she had not come across any good argument that women should *not* have the vote. Although she had come across some women who said: 'I do not want a vote', this was hardly an argument, because how could women 'air a grievance as men could?' It was not the vote that was important, she argued, but the principle behind the vote. Another argument she had heard was that 'if women wanted to have the vote the same as men, they should be prepared to fight the same as men, but that was very stupid'. She also dismissed the idea of women being 'unsexed' as a result, feeling that voting would establish 'comradeship between men and women'. When she mentioned the more familiar argument of women's place being in the home, there was applause from the men at the back, and her response was to ask why women were then allowed to work in factories and workshops, a response which met with more applause – this time from the women. Mr Beecroft then gave his opinion that women's judgment was 'inferior' to that of a man, and another of the men present asked if a suffragette would be willing to 'crawl up a sewer', which he had to do as part of his job. A woman in the front row in a cream dress, with a banner proclaiming 'Votes for Women', responded to this last question by saying that as a nurse she had done far worse things! She also mentioned that men were losing their jobs only because women were being underpaid, which drew more applause. The discussion came to an end, with the resolution carried by thirty votes to eighteen.

Another member of the Women's Freedom League, Miss Sidley, was in Southend a month later, speaking at the Westcliff Institute under the auspices of the Southend Progressive League. The Chairman (Mr Blott) introduced her by saying he had no sympathy with the militant tactics of the suffrage movement, but failed to see why sex should disqualify women from voting. Miss Sidley wanted to talk about the way women struggled to subsist if they were single or widowed (bearing in mind that women outnumbered men in the world at large), and were forced to enter the world of labour. However, their labour was 'placed at disadvantage simply because they were women', just as 'women writers had had to publish under subterfuge'. She referred to the lower average wage of women, and how women had asked quietly, and worked for the vote for forty years, so that now the 'rebellion would never be squashed till women ... were allowed freedom of thought and speech .... If confined to home-life ... women [were denied] a chance to be healthy morally, healthy physically and a happy individual.' When asked, she admitted that the Women's Freedom League was a 'militant' society, and 'we are not ashamed of it. We are proud. We maintain that almost any means are justifiable to protest against the continued slavery of women ... rebellion is the only means by which we can get our desires.' She went on to point out that although the suffrage movement had held 3,000 meetings, they were only heard of when they chained themselves to the grille of the House of Commons. 'It was no joke for women to go to gaol, to be treated as criminals. There was no fun in that; they had women who had gone and gone again … [to] … undertake this degradation and physical and mental suffering.' On being questioned again about militancy, she pointed out that such methods by men would be 'absolutely unjustifiable because they had the constitutional methods. Give women the same – the vote – and they would cease the use of the militant tactics.' She was happy to reply to all the questions thrown at her, arguing that women were equal to men intellectually but were 'superior morally', and reminding the attendees that appealing to the 'justice and gallantry' of men had not worked. What was described as an interesting meeting (with a full account in the *Southend Standard and Essex Weekly Advertiser* of 25 November 1909) ended with a vote in favour of votes for women by two to one.

Similar positive outcomes are also documented at other meetings held in the town – that of the Southend and Westcliff Women's Liberal Association in November 1910 at the Medical Mission Hall in Clarence Road, for instance. Mrs Osborn was in attendance again, this time asking for support for the female vote from speaker Mr Burrows, JP, who said that his vote ought to be given to the women, not to influence voting in the next election, but as a matter of principle. He also said he would use his influence to urge the government to press forward, although he did strike a note of caution when he stressed that the vote should not be used by women as a 'plaything'. The Leigh Debating Society's 1910 speaker was Nellie Martel, working at the time for the WSPU in London, who had been involved in the suffrage movement in Australia from 1891. Such meetings are proof of the suffrage movement spreading its influence throughout a variety of women's organisations in the town.

Mrs Kineton Parkes seems to have struck a chord locally. There was particular local opposition to the idea of women paying tax without having a vote, or a say in how these taxes were spent, and members of the Women's Tax Resistance League demonstrated in Southend in 1912 (probably during the South East Essex by-election in March). They travelled the streets in an open horse and carriage with posters bearing the slogan of the TRL: 'No Vote, No Tax'. The TRL conducted a campaign of organised resistance to taxation, associated with the Women's Freedom League, as a way of protesting against the disenfranchisement of women, believing that taxation and representation should go hand in hand.

One local woman was at the forefront of this particular struggle. This was Mrs Rosa Sky, who ran a confectionery and tobacconists shop in Clifftown Road, Southend. She had been separated from her commercial traveller husband since 1892 when he deserted her and her three surviving children, leaving her with a working-class income but middle-class ideals. She had approached the National Union of Women's Suffrage Societies in London four years earlier (ten years after its inception), suggesting a branch be set up in Southend, but there is no trace of this being formed. This may well be partly due to the fact that her letter (quoted in *The Common Cause* of June 1911) dismisses many local women as being merely 'boarding and lodging house-keepers', and dismissing Southend (incorrectly!) as having no factories or industry. According to Fawcett Library records (now the Women's Library at the London School of Economics), Mrs Sky was apparently ready to take on what she called 'an uphill fight', and she had collected 400 signatures in favour of votes for women which she had sent to the House of Commons (see the *Suffrage Annual and Women's Who's Who* of 1913 which also refers to her taking part in every procession in London including the famous Mud March of 1907, organised by the NUWSS, which, in spite of the foul weather, gave the suffrage movement a sense of respectability that the militant tactics of the Women's Social and Political Union did not).

However, it was a branch of the more militant breakaway WSPU that eventually came to fruition locally, in 1910, Mrs Sky becoming its Treasurer, along with her involvement with the TRL. They had weekly meetings at the Cottage Tea Rooms, then in Nelson Street, as well as in members' homes. The WSPU was a result of the legendary Emmeline Pankhurst's decision to take the suffrage movement away from the middle-class

NUWSS, to young working-class women to draw attention to the cause in a more militant campaign. The members of the local WSPU are listed in the *Southend and Westcliff Graphic* of 15 September 1911:

> Mrs Swift
> Mrs Bull
> Mrs Smith
> Mrs Sky (Hon. Sec.) [note: more likely to have been Treasurer]
> Mrs Gladdy
> Mrs Parrish
> Mrs Warren
> Miss Warren
> Miss Ilsley

(Note the number of married women, compared to the nineteenth-century suffrage movement, which comprised primarily single women – which could be said to indicate some progress.) By 1913, Mrs Sky had handed over her role to Eva Woodthorpe from Oakleigh Park Drive, Leigh-on-Sea. Miss Woodthorpe was one of a number of Southend women who took part in poster parades in Parliament Square, London, before the First World War, and is generally thought to have been imprisoned, although this is unevidenced. There is, however, a cryptic reference to Eva and Irene Woodthorpe being summoned 'for obstructing the footway in Alexandra Street by wheeling their cycles on the path', in June 1902 in the *Essex Newsman*, reporting on proceedings at Southend Police Court. The two women were fined 6*s* each. A suffrage mini-protest under-played by the press? Possibly. The following more detailed story appeared in the *London Standard* of 27 February 1913:

> Four suffragists were roughly handled at Leigh-on-Sea yesterday when they attempted to hold a sandwich board parade. A large crowd had gathered, and, raising the cry 'We'll have no suffragettes in Leigh' they took away the women's boards and

handbills. Two of the women, Mrs Sky and Miss Woodthorpe, were struck and injured, their hats torn off.

It is important to realise that public opinion of militant suffragettes was generally unsupportive and often hostile. They were considered to be a threat to society, destabilising the natural order where women were subordinate. The Primrose League, promoting Conservative principles, with a local branch started in 1914 by Mary Spencer Warren of Leigh-on-Sea, supported the aims of the suffragettes, but not the methods. Even the Southend branch of the Women's Liberal Association passed a resolution – on Friday 15 December 1911, reported in the *Essex County Chronicle* – protesting against the militant methods of suffragettes. Mrs Sky's defiance is personified, in particular, by her 1911 census return when she wrote across the form: 'No votes for women. No information from women.' When she failed to pay her taxes in 1911, 1912 and again in 1914, goods were seized from her home and auctioned locally to raise the necessary funds. Mrs Sky also displayed the additional Notice of Penalty in her shop window. In 1911, the auction at Elam and Sons had been attended by no less than Mrs Kineton-Parkes. Following the auction, according to the *Southend Standard*, a crowd, made up of members of the public from the auction as well as representatives of the WSPU and WTRL, marched along Southchurch Road to Southend Technical College where more speeches were delivered. The article reported on 'a lot of chaff being indulged', as protesters (incidentally including local men, not just women) made their way through the streets. The reporter wrote of proceedings being enthusiastic, with many questions asked. The main Southend WSPU banner had been handpainted by Mr Parrish, whose wife was a member of the local branch.

At the 1914 auction, Mrs Sky's gold and diamond ring was seized (raising £4 10*s*), along with a silver rose bowl from another demonstrator, Mrs Douglas-Hamilton, which raised £4 (*Chelmsford Chronicle*, 3 July 1914). Mrs Hamilton, a wealthy Londoner, had given a convalescent home at Southend for tired workers and their families from the East End to spend holidays, knowing as she did the conditions under which they lived. This was the home – facing the sea and with trees in the back gardens, funded entirely by her own resources – on which she, too, had refused to pay tax for five years as a protest against continued non-representation.

Rosa Sky was one of over 200 women, mostly middle class, who avoided paying their taxes between 1906 and 1918, although the movement was rather deflated by the outbreak of war when the fight for suffrage generally was put on ice. Census evasion was the subject of a meeting at the Masonic Hall in the spring of 1911 and was so well attended that there were insufficient seats. In May 1917, Mrs Sky wrote about her intention to visit London to meet the Women's Franchise Declaration Committee, an organisation formed in 1906, which went on to gather 257,000 signatures from the fields of education, social work, office work, trade and art, resulting in a declaration which was brushed aside by the government, increasing the call for militancy. (Her letter is in the Women's Library, London.)

Various copies of *The Common Cause* in the National Archives at Kew refer to the local WSPU having regular meetings before the First World War, with a strong contingent joining the great London procession of 17 June 1911. The same publication also quotes a Mrs R. S. Hind-Smith of Westcliff, who apparently did not agree that the militant and non-militant societies should walk together, for it would be difficult for people to distinguish between the law abiding and law-breaking – the main militant action locally was non-payment of taxes and chalking the pavements (i.e. early graffiti). There is at least one incident which made the headlines, however, bearing in mind that much militant activity was not in fact reported to discourage the suffragette movement. This was in June 1913 when the *Chelmsford Chronicle* reported that anonymous suffragettes had attempted to destroy St John's Church, alongside the Palace Hotel:

> The interior of the organ was found by the verger to contain a large quantity of unused wax matches,

> carefully piled up. On the top of them were piled about thirty live ball cartridges, oily rags, and other inflammable materials. Lying in the vestry were copies of *The Suffragette* and *Votes for Women*.

Local women supported their peers during the First World War in a variety of ways. One particularly busy female, Mrs Wildman Baker, was the wife of a doctor at the (temporary) hospital in Southchurch Road known as The Glen. She was secretary to the Thorpe Bay branch of the Hospital Aid Working Party, the English Red Cross, the Mine Sweepers, the Ladies Committee of the Glen Hospital, President of the Thorpe Bay Habitation of the Young Helpers' League, President of the Ladies Committee of the Thorpe Hall Golf Club and Chair of the 1st Thorpe Bay Girl Guides (phew!), as well as being a member of the Serbian Relief Fund and the French Red Cross. Support by more well-known women was kept fairly low profile. One example is the author Rebecca West, who moved from London in February 1917 with her 2-year-old son, Anthony, and lived in Southcliffe, Marine Parade, in Leigh-on-Sea for a few years until the Zeppelins overhead and the sounds of warfare drove them away. She had been financially assisted by H. G. Wells, having been his mistress for several years, Anthony being his son. West was a WSPU supporter and marched with Votes for Women groups. Her book *The Sentinel* dates from 1911 and gives a full account of the horror of hunger strikes and imprisonment endured by suffragettes. She also wrote for several suffragette publications including the *Freewoman* and the *Clarion*. H. G. Wells himself was, incidentally, one of the most effective male voices for early feminism, and wrote a novel (*Ann Veronica* – 1909) addressing his support of women winning the right to vote and thereby gaining independence from men.

Women began turning up in the local council minutes as committee members at the beginning of the twentieth century – Mrs Osborn forming part of the Education Committee from November 1903. The first female councillor was elected for Westborough Ward in 1910, i.e., Miss Bannester, the Principal of Alexandra College, who had stood against four men. At the time, she mentioned one man's hurtful comment that a 'woman's place was to act as man's guardian at home, although this could not apply to a middle-aged spinster like herself', and she sat on the Education and Library Committees, promoting education for women. Leigh-on-Sea could boast its first female JP by 1920 – Councillor Adelaide Hawken – with other women having apparently been considered, namely Mrs Steer of the Food Control and Profiteering Committee, and Miss Durrant, a local hairdresser (*Essex Newsman* 13 March 1920.) More female names appear in the 1920s in the annual Southend Yearbook – three on the Maternity and Child Welfare Committee for instance, plus two female magistrates by 1923, and female councillors listed in 1926. This was the year that the first Labour Woman Councillor (Mrs Martha Lilian Edwards) had been voted in, with a majority of seventy-two votes over the male Conservative candidate. Miss M. E. Reay was a JP and had been awarded a CBE by the time she was re-elected Vice-Chairman of the Southend Education Committee in November 1929, a year after women had finally secured the vote for all over the age of 21. By 1932, Southend had its first female candidate for mayor, Councillor Constance Leyland, who had served Milton Ward from February 1926, although it took her another two decades to get the role she obviously coveted. In the meantime, she continued to teach (including life-saving techniques in the swimming pool) at Lindisfarne College in Westcliff-on-Sea. In 1937, she was the only female on the Coronation Committee which organised a string of events in the town including an elaborate historic pageant, and was a great supporter of the repertory movement in Southend before the war, dauntlessly selling shares from the stage to help the movement. She became the first lady Alderman in 1943 and was awarded an MBE in 1946 for her services to Civil Defence as the County Borough organiser for the Southend WVS.

When the Representation of the People Act was passed in 1918, allowing some women over 30 'with property' to vote, it did not make headlines in Southend's newspapers, which were pre-occupied with the end of the war. It is the general view that the granting of the vote for women was the result of the campaigns of the women's suffrage movement, after the delay caused by war. Another view is that giving some women the vote was seen as a compromise to granting all women the vote. There is evidence to suggest that the Act was passed to avoid a return to the violent protests of the suffragettes. It would have been embarrassing for the government to go back to arresting and imprisoning women, subjecting them to humiliation and force feeding, when they had done so much for the war effort.

In spite of such progress, it was not until 1927, that Gwendolen Guinness, Lady Iveagh, the wife of the long-serving Conservative MP for Southend, came to prominence. She had been the Chair of the Women's Advisory Committee of the Conservative Central Office since 1918 and since 1925 had had a role in the Women's Unionist Organisation as well as campaigning for her husband in nine campaigns stretching back to 1912. When he stood down in 1927, she took on the constituency herself, becoming one of the first female MPs in the UK and joining only a handful of others in the House of Commons. Lady Iveagh supported Prime Minister Stanley Baldwin, who proposed equal parliamentary voting rights for women despite opposition from those to the right of his party, and she was an ardent supporter of his Equal Franchise Act, which finally granted equal voting rights to men and women at 21. It is perhaps unfortunate, nevertheless, that when she attended the House of Commons, fellow male MPs would crowd in mainly to see her fashionable clothes. But she must have been delighted to find that the local electorate from 1928 became predominantly women, which continued right through until at least 1935, the year she retired from parliament. (In the meantime, Lady Iveagh had been involved, with her husband, in the Overseas Training School in Surrey, extending its reach to women from 1914, to prepare them for settlement in the colonies by learning poultry-rearing, cookery and preserving.)

The *Essex Chronicle* quoted Viscountess Elveden's comment at a meeting of the Women's Unionist Association in Southend in October 1921 that 'the success of the meeting showed that in Essex [women] were not drowned in apathy as some would have them believe'. However, there does not seem to have been much celebrating in Southend in 1928 following the extending of the vote to all women over 21, although Mrs Boyce, at another Women's Unionist Meeting in Southend in November 1928, did make an interesting comment on the subject. She is also quoted in the *Chelmsford Chronicle* as saying: 'When I am told by people that it is an absurd thing to give girls the vote because they will only vote as their sweethearts do, I reply at once – don't believe it. I believe it will more likely be the other way round.' (The Women's Unionists had gradually taken over from the Primrose League.) Suffrage was not the only cause supported by local women. In September 1926, eight women from the Southend branch of the National Unemployed Workers' Movement marched to a demonstration in nearby Rayleigh, singing the Red Flag en route, with another contingent – including ten local women – marching to London in 1934 to parade in Hyde Park. This new era for women, which would redefine the relationship between women and men generally, not just politically, did get a mention in the *Essex Chronicle* of 15 June 1928, when a meeting of the often quoted Southend Women's Liberal Association at Woodford Lodge, Victoria Avenue, was chaired by the prospective Liberal candidate, the Hon. Dougal Meston. He confirmed the importance of the women's vote to the electorate. He quoted figures of 54,000 voters in Southend, of which 25,000 had been women, the latter figure having increased to 31,000 women as a result of the 1928 act. He was no doubt optimistic that many of these extra 6,000 votes would be for the Liberal party.

Between the wars was a time for women to make some progress with their lives in Southend. When the suffrage movement spawned the Townswomen's Guild in 1929, after women had won the right to vote, its ongoing aim was to educate women about good citizenship. They continued to campaign for women to use their vote wisely as well as promoting ties between women in rural areas, with the WI its urban equivalent. A local branch at Leigh opened in 1930, followed by what appears to have been a further Westcliff and Leigh branch a year later. The Guild has often lobbied on national and local issues, giving women the opportunity to develop new skills, campaign on various issues, support each other, make new friends and above all, have fun. The efforts of women in the town were not always acknowledged, as when Rotarian Mr J. H. Burrows referred to the Ladies Auxiliary raising £50 for charity in 1938, which was handed over to the Men's Fund for Distribution and Works, meaning that the menfolk got the credit. At this same meeting (reported in the *Southend Standard*), he did propose a toast to the ladies who he described as 'the good looking Southend ladies' – perhaps he hoped that might help. Meetings of the Guild in the 1940s were held in various locations (including the Druids Hall in Eastern Avenue), with local papers describing their ongoing involvement – even though the vote was won – in such activities as ballroom dancing and knitting, but supporting their sisters in more worthy causes when necessary.

As always, it was the middle-class women who were prominent in Southend in the first half of the twentieth century. Gertrude Mouillot, a music hall artiste and actress, lost her husband in 1911 and was left with a fortune including fifteen theatres. She added the Palace Theatre in Westcliff to her collection in 1920, eight years after it was built, attracting big names such as Ivor Novello and Ralph Richardson, thanks to her theatrical connections. (It was not rare for a woman to own a theatre; there was an early theatre in the town, Trotters, owned by a Mrs Susannah Clarke in 1859, according to *Southend Playhouses from 1793*.) After a difficult time for theatres in the 1930s, she decided – in 1942 – to give it to the people of Southend. This reflected her interest in, and goodwill for, the town and was a gift for the benefit of the people, with a caveat to ensure it was not put up for sale and that it was made available for amateur performances. Gertrude had apparently always been interested in politics and in feminism, and offered some of her work as a playwright for the benefit of suffragette campaigns. She is believed to have been a member of the Actresses' Franchise League, an organisation founded in 1908 in support of the suffrage movement. (She died in 1961, aged 94, in Colchester – close to a town in which she had never lived, but which continues to benefit from her generosity.)

When Lady of the Manor of South Shoebury, Margaret Knapping (daughter of brickfield magnate Dale Knapping) died in 1935, her legacy was more concerned with culture than community, as she left the bulk of her fortune to the Tate Gallery in London. However, during her lifetime, she acquired a feisty reputation, described as an eccentric who gambled on horses, painted, played golf and polo, and took a younger lover – Liberal MP Lord Strabolgi. Generally, women like Margaret Knapping, although approving of the gradual successes that struggling women were having in achieving some of their rights, were onlookers more than participants. Having said that, there is just one – fascinating – reference following her death in, of all things, an Australian newspaper (*The Horsham Times*), which describes Margaret as having been 'in the heyday of her youth … a keen suffragette'!

Local women during the Second World War made active contributions in various ways (see Chapter Two), but for national rather than women's causes. But they were back on the case by 1946 when Alderman Constance Leyland presided over the October inaugural luncheon of the Southend and District Business and Professional Women's Club at Garons in the High Street. The mayor spoke of the commendable attributes that professional and business women in Southend could bring, furthering interest in the town. Referring to the local elections, he pointed out that only twenty-three per cent (men and women) went to the polls, and women were needed to show an interest in the town's affairs, with the club offering a real benefit to Southend, to the country and 'eventually to the rest of the world'! Alderman Leyland said that members wanted a first-class club to work from the women's angle, side-by-side with the men's organisations, as per the *Southend Standard* of 19 October 1946. Three years later, 400 women delegates from all over Britain met at the Palace Hotel to urge the Minister of Health to impress upon local authorities the need for accommodation for single people and to secure 'for spinsters' the same 1949 'resident housekeeper allowance free of income tax at present enjoyed by widows and widowers'. The mayor's predictions could be said to be slowly coming to fruition ... although women nationally had to wait until 1970 for the Equal Pay Act of course, and until the 1980s before being admitted to the main bar of the Naval and Military Club in Royal Terrace which had been in existence since the 1920s.

There are a couple of other local women that should be singled out for attention for their breakaway from stereotype. One was Dorothy Coke, who had studied art during the First World War, preparing her for her work as a war artist on the British home front during the next war. She depicted the work being performed by women in various services, spending time with the WVS, the ATS, the WAAF and Red Cross. Then there was the ex-student of Southend High School who became the organising secretary for the Keep Left Group, formed in 1947. This was Jo Richardson, a socialist and active trade unionist, who had become involved in politics initially as a secretary to MP Ian Mikardo, but who went on to become an MP herself in the 1970s. In the 1940s and beyond, she was well known for her flaming red hair, but more so as a champion of women's rights, and her feminism was based on 'all the women with expertise and wisdom who never get to first base; they're poor, they've got kids ... their lives are drudgery' – influenced by her own mother's financial struggles. The prominence of women's causes within the Labour Party is largely due to Jo Richardson's campaigning as one of what the *Independent* called: 'the dynamos of the Left in Britain'. (2 February 1994.)

However, in Southend as elsewhere, a new era was evolving by 1950. Women were demonstrating their capability of fighting for their freedoms, breaking down barriers and exploding male theories about them. It had taken three generations of British feminists to win the most basic civil rights for women – the right to an education, to keep their own earnings and to vote. What was happening was beyond the wildest dreams of the early Victorians, suffragettes or not, all over Essex and all over the UK.

Bibliography

Barber, John, *Coleman Street's Children,* self-published, 1999

Benton, Philip, *The History of Rochford Hundred,* A. Harrington, 1888

Bright, Mary, *Days of Our Lives*, Harknett Heritage Publishing, 2010

Burrows, J.W., *Southend-on-Sea & District,* John H. Burrows & Sons, Southend-on-Sea, 1909

Carmichael, Harry, *With Future and With Past,* Southend High School for Boys, 1995

Crowe, Ken, *Kursaal Memories,* Skelter Publishing, St Alban's, 2003

Davenport, Jim, and Foster, Rodney, *Thorpe Hall Golf Club 1907–2007*, Thorpe Hall Golf Co. Ltd, 2007

Dilley, Roy, *Southend's Palaces of the Silver Screen,* Phillimore & Co. Ltd. Andover, 2011

Drury, John, *Essex Workhouses,* Farthings Publications, Felsted, 2006

Edwards, Carol, *The High Street Southend on Sea,* self-published, 2016

Edwards, Carol, *Seaside Entrepreneurs,* self-published, 2010

Edwards, Carol, *The Life & Times of the Houseboats of Leigh-on-Sea,* self-published, 2009

Edwards, Carol, *The Old Town, Leigh-on-Sea,* self-published, 2013

Everritt, Sylvia, *Southend Seaside Holiday,* Phillimore & Co. Ltd, Chichester, 1980

Finch, Peter, *Voluntary Hospitals of Southend-on-Sea 1887–1948,* Southend-on-Sea General Hospital, 1948

Glennie, Donald, *Our Town,* Civic Publications Southend-on-Sea, 1947

Goodale, Alfred, *Holy Trinity Southchurch,* no publisher information, 1974

Goodale, A. *Southchurch: A History of a Parish,* Industrial Press, Southend on Sea, c. 1950

Gordon, Dee, *The Secret History of Southend-on-Sea,* The History Press, Stroud, 2014

Gordon, Dee, *Southend at War,* The History Press, Stroud, 2010

Hadden, Stephanie, *What an Education,* West Leigh Junior School, 2003

Jefferies, Malcolm, and Lee, J. Alfred, *The Hospitals of Southend,* Phillimore & Co. Chichester, 1986

Jerram-Burrows, Lily E., *The History of Rochford Hundred (South Shoebury),* Rochford Hundred Historical Society, 1978

Jerram-Burrows, Lily E., *The History of Rochford Hundred (Shopland),* Rochford Hundred Historical Society, 1978

Jerram-Burrows, Lily E., *Rochford Remembers,* Rochford Hundred Historical Society, 1983

Keen, Bertha (Compiler), *Tales Out of School,* Southend High School for Girls, 1975

King, Tom and Furbank, Kevan, *The Southend Story,* Southend Standard Recorder/Southend-on-Sea Borough Council Marketing Department, 1991

Mansell, Pam and Foster, Rebecca, *The Girls of Southend High School 1913–2013,* Matador, Leicestershire, 2013

McSean, Denis, *Southend Hospital 1885–1995,* Southend Health Care NHS Trust, 1995

Melling, John Kennedy, *Southend Playhouses from 1793,* Essex Countryside, Letchworth 1969

Newby, Jennifer, *Women's Lives*, Pen & Sword Books Ltd, Barnsley, 2011

Orfeur, M. *Alexandra College 1892–1959,* self-published, 1985

Orford, Maureen, *The Shoebury Story,* Ian Henry Publications, Romford, 2000

Pearce, Marion, *Milton, Chalkwell & The Crowstone,* Ian Henry Publications, Romford, 2000

Pewsey, Stephen, *The Book of Southend-on-Sea*, Baron Birch, 1993

Phillips, Melanie, *The Ascent of Woman,* Little, Brown, London, 2003

Poole, Chris and Brown, Peter, *Ekco Sounds,* Estuary Publishing, Southend, 2013

Rayner, Albert, *The Rayner Family of Great Wakering,* self-published, c.1990

Reynolds, Dr David, *Old Rochford Hospital,* Cambridge Press, 1995

Sipple, Mavis, *Prittlewell: A History,* JTT Publishing, 2008

Tait, Lynn, (Compiler) *The Tatler,* (Special Edition to celebrate 75th Anniversary of Chalkwell Hall Schools), 1984

Tawke, Augusta, *Recollections of Southend-on-Sea,* 1915, but self-published, 1936

Tawke, Augusta, *Hunting Recollections,* Francis & Sons, Rochford, 1913

U3A/Leigh Society Shared Learning Project, *Letters from Leigh,* the Leigh Society, 2017

Watkins, Rueda, and Rodriguez, *Introducing Feminism,* Totem Books NY, 1994

Further reading:

Where To Buy At Southend, Robinson, Son & Pike, Brighton, 1891

Mates Illustrated Guide to Southend on Sea, Southend-on-Sea Corporation, 1907

Derbyshire's Guide to Southend-on-Sea, 1901

Kelly's Directories

Hatton's Southend-on-Sea Guide and Directory, 1904–5

Echoes, the EKCO Staff Magazines, 1930s

The Common Cause, 1910–1917

St Mary's Prittlewell Magazines, 1920s & 1930s

A Momentous Century: Wesley Methodist Church, Leigh-on-Sea 1897–1997, unauthored

Southend Council Minutes 1892–1920

Suffrage Annual and Women's Who's Who, ed. A.J.R., Stanley Paul, London, 1913

British Newspaper Archive (on line)

Index